THE LIVING PRESENCE
OF THE PAST

A. M. ALLCHIN

THE LIVING PRESENCE
OF THE PAST

THE DYNAMIC OF
CHRISTIAN TRADITION

The Seabury Press · New York

1981
The Seabury Press
815 Second Avenue
New York, N.Y. 10017

Library of Congress Cataloging in Publication Data

Allchin, A. M.
The living presence of the past.

1. Tradition (Theology) 2. Church—Unity.
3. Continuity of the Church. 4. Prayer. I. Title.
BT90.A46   230   81-5692
ISBN 0-8164-2334-2   AACR2

Contents

Preface

The central section of this book consists of the Margaret Harris Lectures given in the University of Dundee in April 1979. I am grateful to the authorities of the University for their invitation to be the Margaret Harris Lecturer for that year, and to my friends in the city and university for their generous welcome during my stay there. An invitation to lecture at Nashotah House, Wisconsin, in the spring of 1980 gave me the opportunity to rework some of this material and to develop further points of special transatlantic concern. While I have in some places expanded the original text of the lectures I have not tried to disguise the form of the spoken word.

I have added to these chapters an introduction which looks at some of the underlying convictions which run through this book, and which link it to two previous books which I have published, and an epilogue which carries into greater detail themes touched on in chapters three and four and looks further into the mystery of Christian worship with which the whole book is concerned. This concluding chapter also had a Scottish origin, having grown from a lecture given in Edinburgh and Aberdeen in November 1978, at the invitation of the Church Service Society. An earlier version appeared in the Society's journal, *The Liturgical Review*. I wish to thank all those, both in Scotland and in the United States of America, whose interest and kindness has been a stimulus to further thought. I wish to thank the Sisters of the Love of God, Fairacres, Oxford, for their constant support.

To the Father Abbot and the brethren of the Abbey of Ste Marie du Mont, I owe an increasing debt of gratitude. By welcoming me time and again to share in their life of prayer and silence they have provided the conditions which made possible the writing of this book.

A. M. Allchin
December 1980   Canterbury

Acknowledgements

Thanks are due to the following for permission to reproduce extracts from copyright sources:

Darton, Longman & Todd Ltd and University of California Press: *The Vedic Experience* by Raimundo Panikkar.
Faber & Faber Ltd: 'The Transfiguration' from *Collected Poems of Edwin Muir* by Edwin Muir. Excerpts from *Four Quartets* by T. S. Eliot, copyright 1943 by T. S. Eliot; renewed 1971 by Esme Valerie Eliot, used by permission also of Harcourt Brace Jovanovich Inc.
Penguin Books Ltd: *Piers the Ploughman* by William Langland translated by J. F. Goodridge (Penguin Classics, Revised edition 1966) pp. 36, 131–3, 218–9, 221–3, 226–8.
Random House, Inc: *The Pearl Poet: His Complete Works* translated by Margaret Williams R.S.C.J. Copyright © 1967 by Margaret Williams R.S.C.J.
University of Wales Press: *Presenting Saunders Lewis* edited by Alun R. Jones and Gwyn Thomas.

Introduction

This is a book which is concerned with the question of unity, and specifically with the question of the unity of Christendom. The subject, however, is not envisaged primarily in terms of Church structures or disputed doctrines, though those things are not wholly ignored, but in terms of a unity of faith and experience, a continuity of prayer and life through the centuries, a vision of the wholeness and coherence of all things. The unity of the Church is considered here insofar as the Church is seen as a sign and sacrament of the unity of mankind, and of the reconciliation of man with God, his neighbour and himself. 'Things fall apart, the centre cannot hold': W. B. Yeats' words must be amongst the most frequently quoted of our century. That fact itself witnesses to the powerful sense of disintegration which afflicts our society. In this book we try to see a little of what would be implied by the Christian affirmation that all things finally hold together in one.

In particular the book is concerned more with the question of unity in time than in space, with what the poet and painter David Jones has called 'the inward continuities' which link apparently divided centuries. Like T. S. Eliot, David Jones was one who saw clearly the necessity of tradition for the work of the writer or the artist. In another field, one of the greatest Eastern Orthodox theologians of our time, Fr George Florovsky, stressed the same point. He was in the habit of speaking of the need for 'an ecumenism in time', a serious exchange, an active encounter between the Church of today and the Church of former ages. That is what we seek to explore in these pages; the possibility of emerging from the parochialism of our own period, and the liberty which comes from being able to live alongside men and women of other epochs and other civilizations than our own. The questions raised touch the vital matter of the Church's relationship to the events from which it takes its origin. How can it be true that we become contemporaries of the Gospel events? What does it mean to say that we hold the same faith as those who have preceded us by so many centuries? Voices have not been lacking within the theological world which have questioned very radically the possibility of any real unity of faith and experience across the gulfs which separate our post-critical world from earlier ages.

Linked to these larger questions is another set of problems about the way in which tradition functions. If we allow that there is some real continuity of life and thought, how is it maintained? Do we remain true to the past by refusing to change, or by being willing to change? How is it that a tradition seems at times able to renew itself from within? As a distinguished American philosopher of religion, John E. Smith, puts it: 'what is it that has the power to unify many selves and to sustain that unity in a living way so that we pass beyond abstract unity and reach a constant unifying power which is the form of life itself?' [1] Can we say that it is the Holy Spirit who is the bearer and creator of the tradition? Is it perhaps more helpful to speak of certain archetypal patterns in the heart and mind of men which have their own inherent vitality? Shall we have need of both ways of approach if we are to do justice to the mystery of human creativity when the freedom of man is touched and energized by the activity of God?

At the heart of this process of tradition, there stands the practice of prayer in its many forms, hidden and personal, public and corporate, spontaneous and ecstatic, ordered and ceremonial. All of them provide ways by which the past is linked with the present and the present opened to the future, because all of them bring the world of time into touch with the world of eternity. In all of them the idea of *anamnesis* is to be found, the memory of God and the memory of what God has done. This is one of the constant themes of this book, and from time to time our attention focuses on the life and witness of communities who make the practice of prayer the centre and purpose of their life, for they can show us, in a vivid and concentrated way, things that are true for all those who take

2

prayer seriously in their lives. Their habit of turning their backs on the world in order to discover God is found, by a healing paradox, to have surprisingly positive results for the understanding and appreciation of this world as God's creation. Their cultivation of the art of contemplation gives us a clue to a radical re-appraisal of our attitude to things. Unexpected powers of cognition are released when the minds of men and women are constantly turned towards the reality of God's eternal Kingdom as it enters into time.

The practice of prayer proves to be not only or even primarily a matter of giving comfort to the emotions, or providing stimulus to the will, but of bringing light and understanding to the mind, providing serious illumination of man's relationship with God, and of his situation in this world in which he finds himself. The recovery of the neglected arts of prayer and contemplation may be necessary to us, if we are to find ways to correct the disastrous imbalances of our society. There are clues here which point towards the possibility of growth and change into the future. To illustrate this point it may be useful to concentrate our attention for a moment on one particular person, and we could hardly do better than to to take by way of example the case of the fourteenth-century mystic Julian of Norwich.

I

The writings of Julian of Norwich may be said to have entered into the mainstream of English literature at that moment in 1943 when T. S. Eliot quoted from *The Revelations of Divine Love* in the last of his *Four Quartets*, *Little Gidding*. The words which Eliot chose from her book: 'Sin is behovely, but all shall be well and all shall be well and all manner of thing shall be well' are, in themselves, a remarkable affirmation of a final ultimate reconciliation and unity. They stand very close to the heart of her book, and evidently they have spoken in a particular way to men and women of our own time. For in the years since Eliot's poem was written her work has become, at least in Britain, one of the best known of all English medieval spiritual writings. This popularity of Julian in the second half of the twentieth century is a remarkable phenomenom. In her

3

own time her work seems to have been very little known. Compared with that of other spiritual writers of her century, with Richard Rolle and Walter Hilton for example, manuscripts of her work are very few. In the first part of our own century her book began to be more widely known, but primarily among the devout.[2] It was read more as a book of devotion, tender, moving and vivid, than as a work of much intellectual content or rigour. Only in recent years have scholars begun to look at Julian not only as a writer of compassion, but as a writer of wisdom. Thus we have had the first major critical edition of her work, and two major academic studies of it, one primarily theological, the other more linguistic and literary.[3] All the scholars concerned consider Julian to be a great theologian, one who reflected long and deeply on the mysteries of Christian faith, a woman of much learning as well as a woman of much intuition, who shows a remarkable balance and judgement in the treatment of her subject. She is one whose mind is acute and accurate as well as sensitive and imaginative. She is a writer who not only recapitulates the tradition which she had inherited from the past but who in many ways anticipates in a prophetic fashion some of the urgently felt theological issues of our time. We might give as examples her concept of the Motherhood of God, or her understanding of the sacredness of the earth and of man's bodily nature. In her we sense a startling presence of the past.

We ought not to underestimate the strangeness of these convictions about the importance of a life given to prayer, nor the amazement which they would have brought to the great majority of our ancestors during the last four hundred years, and indeed would still bring to most of our contemporaries now. To a well-educated Englishman of the seventeenth, eighteenth or nineteenth century, it would have seemed mere folly to suppose that an uneducated woman of the middle ages, living the restricted and unnatural life of a hermit, would have been able to give us any serious illumination on the predicament of man or the nature of God. Monks and nuns were creatures of the past, of an age which had vanished forever. This, of course, would primarily have been the case for those of us who come from the traditions which went through the experience of the Reformation in the sixteenth century.

But not only for them. It is true that in English Roman Catholicism there has been a long and honourable tradition of concern for the medieval spiritual writers of our land, a tradition which was maintained through the years of persecution; it was Father Augustine Baker and his disciples in the seventeenth century who preserved for us the work of Julian and her contemporaries. But even Roman Catholics have not been able to escape the influence of the spirit of the age, and that spirit has been very powerful, whether manifest as the rationalism of the eighteenth, the activism of the nineteenth, or the belief in progress of the early twentieth century, and in none of its forms has it shown much regard for a life of solitude and contemplation. How marginal, for instance, does the spiritual writer William Law in his retreat at Kingscliffe seem to be to the public concerns of eighteenth century England. All of us have suffered more than we know from the conviction, assumed rather than stated, that man can learn only by going outward, and that serious wisdom can only be gained in universities, or in the field of public action.

Our whole civilization, in its unspoken and unquestioned assumptions and attitudes is opposed, not so much to the individual contemplating, any more than it is opposed to the individual singing or writing poetry, as to any evaluation of the contemplative act, whether in a religious or artistic form which would place it at the heart and apex of human life and society. Our world says: 'You may do it as long as you recognize that it is something which is not really important'; and as both the artist and the man or woman of prayer knows, this is the one condition which makes their work impossible. Here the contrast between our own time and the middle ages is particularly sharp.

Julian of Norwich, for instance, was an integral part of a society which seriously regarded her way of life as the most important, the most valuable of callings. She was a citizen of a city which put at its centre a cathedral, not because it was thought that it would make a beautiful addition or adornment to a society which had already been constructed, but because men believed that worship and prayer were the most vital and necessary of all human activities. One only has to begin to live with such a building to sense how little we understand of its full meaning for those who built it, and to feel how much our civilization, in gaining technical and scientific knowledge, has lost in understanding of the meaning and symbolism of space and architecture, and how it can illuminate human life. We could, if we were minded to, build two or three perfect replicas of Norwich or Canterbury Cathedral, but they would not mean what the original buildings mean because they would not be related to our world in the way in which the originals were related to theirs. They would be artificial, dead things, conveying meanings which we neither understand nor foresee.

Could we reproduce the life of Lady Julian? There are those who live as she did, in solitude and silence, entering day by day into the mystery of God's revelation of himself in Christ, his imparting of himself in the Spirit, and their lives at times bear fruit of the kind and quality which we see in her. But they live in a situation which is so different from hers that it is hardly surprising that they find themselves constantly having to adapt, and to adapt drastically the teaching and tradition which comes from the past. She was part of a monastic civilization which believed that inner work was more important than outer work, which believed than man was made to know and love God, and that this knowledge, though it is mediated through our relationships with our fellow men, is given and grows pre-eminently through the work of prayer and silence, of sacrament and social worship, and through a whole series of activities which our world has banished to the outermost margin of its attention. Our world does not give that priority to the unseen.

Of course, there have not been lacking during the last two centuries those who have looked back to the Middle Ages and to the early Christian centuries for inspiration, and who have thought to find in the organic society of pre-Reformation Europe a kind of model for future development. Undoubtedly, the monastic element in that medieval society has exerted a strong fascination for many people. The most powerful manifestation of this impulse in England was connected with the movement which began in Oxford in the 1830's, and which is associated with the names of Newman, Keble and Pusey. It was a movement which did much to transform both the Roman Catholic community and the established church in this country. Such movements have often been called reactionary and escapist. They had within them, it is true, elements which were purely nostalgic, which sought to escape out of the problems of the nineteenth or twentieth century into the supposed calm of an

6

earlier age. But the fact that there were elements of illusion within them, need not blind us to the elements of truth which they also contained, to their perception that we need to be freed from the temporal parochialism which shuts us up in the assumptions of our own particular era, and to their intuition that we can find in earlier ages some necessary counter-balance to the excessive activism of our own time.

We may well see in some of the counter-cultural movements of the last twenty five years, the latest manifestations of this current of reaction. Only now there are significant differences. Young people have tended to feel more sharply cut off than did their romantic predecessors of the nineteenth century. On the one side there is a much more serious breakdown of confidence in the cultural, political and religious institutions which we have inherited in Western Europe and North America. The reasons for this are not hard to find. The twentieth century has known at the heart of our civilization a resurgence of patterns of brutality, violence and the use of torture, which no one had foreseen at the beginning of this century. The fact of the concentration camps places a very large question mark, to say no more, against the human and moral claims of our society. On the other hand, there is the immense and still accelerating technological revolution, which is increasing man's power over the planet almost beyond belief, and confronting us with problems of a kind that man has never had to face before, and which we often seem frighteningly unwilling to envisage.

It is hardly surprising that there is a widespread feeling that little is to be gained from the study of the past. For some there seems to have been an almost complete break in the sense of continuity with our immediate history. But while there is a widespread disillusionment with the past, there is also a widespread fascination with it. Only now it is not so much the past of our own civilization which attracts people, as the past of others; or if it is our own past, it is its remoter and more nearly mythological regions. Religiously the young have turned instinctively, not to Christianity, but to the teachings of other religions; judging, understandably if wrongly, that the contemplative knowledge and experience which they feel that their world requires cannot be found in Christianity, which is too closely associated with the horrors of our time and has itself become a victim of the spirit of activism which rules our age. In this book we shall explore the fact that the Christian tradition contains within itself a contemplative dimension, a fact of which our contemporaries are often wholly unaware. At the same time we shall applaud the universalism of view of the young, which refuses any longer to be shut in within a single historical experience, or a single historical era. It is God himself, we may believe, who is placing before all the churches, the question of the relation to Christ of all the religious traditions of mankind.

In such a situation, we need a drastic re-appraisal of the culture in which we live. Nothing less than a radical change of vision and perception can save Western man from the sense of inner frustration and emptiness which constantly attacks him, and from the outer threats which that inward emptiness causes. The ecological perils which we face can hardly be resolved without a complete change in our sense of priorities and values and of the meaning of life. This change will mean that man in his solitude, and man in society, will no longer look for his primary fulfilment to the acquisition of more material goods and the extension of his physical power, but to an inner growth of love and knowledge, of vision and understanding, which while it is not unrelated to external conditions, is more than a little independent of them. The contemplative life as it is lived today in continuity with its earlier traditions within the Christian world may be of help to us in making this re-appraisal, presenting us with another vision of things, and another way of living and understanding human life.

If we are to make this radical re-appraisal, we shall have to ask ourselves again why there has been in our Western civilization for the last four centuries, such unrelenting hostility to the contemplative life, and in particular, to the monastic institutions which express and safeguard its central tradition. Such institutions have for centuries been under attack for a great variety of explicit reasons; first of all, at the time of the Reformation in the countries of Protestant Europe, then during the enlightenment in the Catholic countries as well; then again in France and Spain at the end of the last century and the beginning of this; in Russia at the time of Peter the Great, in Greece and the Balkans in the years of national liberation in the nineteenth century, and in the Eastern European countries with renewed vigour following the advent of communist regimes. It may well be that similar conflicts will develop in the

Far East, in Japan, or Burma, or Sri Lanka, in reaction to the monastic traditions of those lands. The Chinese communist destruction of the monastic institutions of Tibet, perhaps the last human society to be modelled consistently around the contemplative life, must also be seen in relation to this whole tradition of hostility to the life of contemplation.

All this has not been by chance. The explicit reasons given for the destruction of these institutions have varied, but underneath there seems to be a consistent story. Our civilization as it has developed has felt itself menaced by a way of life which stood for the complete subversion of its foundation values. It could not feel secure until the very buildings which symbolized that way of life had been destroyed. And now, when many young people are looking for the subversion and overthrow of the values of *our* technical society, they instinctively turn to the monastic figures of the East for guidance, and they try, in a great variety of ways, often baffled and frustrated, to recreate places of contemplation and common life. Not only in California but in Kent people search for ways of rediscovering the inner experience of life. They do not usually think of turning to the Christian tradition for assistance, for they are not aware that it can be of help to them. They do however look for new ways of seeing things, and new ways of living.

What does the Christian monastic tradition have to say in this situation? What kind of insight can it bring? One of the basic questions which it puts to us is about the nature of space and time. We can see this very clearly in the life of a contemplative monastic community. In such a community people decide to stay in one place; they abstain from travelling; they abstain from most of what are regarded as useful forms of work. They involve themselves in a constant round of repetitive acts of worship; they make a radical change of direction in their life. What is true of an enclosed community is even more evidently true in the case of a man or woman who lives such a life of enclosure in solitude, that is to say, in the case of a hermit.

Let us consider Julian of Norwich once again. In such a life as hers space is contracted to a single room, and time stands still; outwardly speaking nothing ever happens. What, we should think, could be more sterile than this? Yet we find as we read her writing, the exact reverse is true. Her book is an affirmation of the potential

9

meaning and extent of human space and human time. When man's life can expand into its true dimension, when it is taken up into God, then one room can contain all the universe, and one life-time can contain all human history. There is here a vital clue to understanding our question about the nature and possibility of unity through the ages. All this Julian sees and knows. She knows that all men are as one man, that one man is as all. She sees in the passion of Christ in which she participates, all the suffering that ever was; the whole drama of man is summed up in one point. And when she speaks to us, we find that she speaks to us as our contemporary.

This fact is in no way peculiar to her. Such a belief about space and time is implicit in the whole tradition of Christian prayer as it is lived in all its many different ways. There is as Eliot says 'a still point' which is at the centre of the turning world. It is also implicit in the whole Christian tradition of faith in Jesus of Nazareth as the one Son of God. One reason why that faith seems impossible to many at the present time is because this fact has not been clearly recognized. The idea that there is a unique incarnation, that three hours' suffering of one man on a certain afternoon in the first century in Palestine 'takes away the sin of the world', can only make sense within a very different view of the nature of things from that which we live with in our everyday existence. It implies the view that all men are indeed summed up, included in one man.

One of the supreme meanings which the solitary life embodies in the Christian tradition is the identification of the solitary with those three hours on the cross. The anchorites and recluses of medieval England took a more hidden way of accepting that identification than the pillar saints of the Christian East, whose mounting of their columns was seen as a direct consequence of and response to their Lord's mounting of the cross. But the reality was no less there. They were to be identified with Jesus in his outward powerlessness and restriction in order that in and through them, as through him, the power to restore life and freedom might be set free. And in this, they were only doing, in a very particular way, what every Christian, indeed what every human being, is called to do in one way or another, to let the mystery of the cross became real and central in one's life.

To see time and space in this way already begins to open up a new way of understanding our relationship with one another, and our relationship with the past. Men may dwell in one another, in ways which our civilization does not expect. The bonds between us are more intimate than we usually recognize. The barrier of death itself is of a different kind from what we usually take it to be. As Eliot puts it, 'The communication of the dead is tongued with fire beyond the language of the living.' The doctrine of the Communion of Saints gives us a new way of appropriating our own history and finding that the past is accessible to us in the present. The purely linear view of time, which has its undeniable uses, can be a great hindrance to an appreciation of the true nature of personal development, or of the true nature of our relationship to the past, to our tradition as a whole. As Thomas MacFarland remarks in his masterly study of Coleridge: 'Chronology can often have a specific value, but its reverence by the scholarly tradition is largely a convention of that tradition complementing the scholarly prejudice that requires "development" in the sense of progressive steps. The text books exult in the proliferation of developmental stages; but such stages do not allow us to see clearly the unfolding of a single, constant orientation to life. Though the data of the world change for us, and their connections with our understanding, the eyes looking out from our time-eroded bodies are the lights of a soul that does not change. Who is to say that the bloom is more truly the flower than is the bud?' [4]

If we suppose for an instant that the great contemplatives are the eyes of a people, then indeed we may think that the life of such a one as Julian of Norwich still gives a single, constant orientation to the whole family to which she belongs; that is to say, in the first place, the whole human family; and then, in the second place, that part of it which acknowledges the reality of redemption, i.e. the Church, and then in the third place, that smaller human family, the people of England, into which she was born. And if this is true of one, how much more it is true of a whole community, or a group of communities, like, for instance, the monasteries of Mount Athos in the heart of Eastern Christendom, or the monasteries of the Cistercian Order in the heart of our Western Christian world. As Fr Andrei Scrima, a distinguished Romanian monk and scholar, remarks: 'Those who have embraced this life of prayer have renounced their part in the public affairs of the world in order to serve the world better, to preserve within it until the end, the invocation of God which must never cease. . . . They should be recognized for what they are; the dead of God, those wounded by Love and Light, who have effaced themselves in the world in order to see the face of the Invisible, from whom they receive their new life.' [5] They withdraw in order to serve; they die in order to receive a new life, which is not theirs alone, but which communicates itself to all who will draw near to them.

Just as the vertical lines of the towers of Norwich or Lincoln or Canterbury Cathedral not only negate but also reaffirm the horizontal lines of the shops and houses which surround them, so too the radical renunciations involved in this way of life prove in the end to have a dramatically life-affirming power. What Philip Sherrard writes about Constantinople is true of every medieval city, every city which has placed at its heart the life of worship: 'So through such submission; through such ascetic renunciation and withdrawal; through such unsleeping vigilance and prayer; through this constant negation, here at the heart of the earthly city . . . of this city's very self, through this whole effort to purify and transcend, was the restless unremitting desire to keep bright the image of the other city, the heavenly Jerusalem, pursued. Relic and holy cult; icon and living saint: these were the instruments, something of whose celestial radiance might be received by whoever with fear, faith and love would move towards them; through them might be stirred and nourished that sense of the sacred, that sense of the presence of a sustaining, transfiguring power by which alone the earthly city might be preserved from the inhuman and vicious compulsions which might otherwise dominate it.' [6]

Insights such as these begin to bring us closer to understanding the power of the life of prayer, the power of a Mother Julian, to attract and to stir us. We begin to become aware in a new way not only of what separates her age from ours, but of what can unite us in the 'unfolding of a single, constant orientation of life'. We begin to feel something of the living and eternal presence of such a past within our present moment, and to discover it as a life-giving presence. All this is not without importance in our search to understand the unity which the Spirit of God can bring to human life, both personal and corporate. It has a distinct bearing on the possibility that we might find within the fragmented history of the

Christian family strands which can unite men and women across the most stubbornly held theological and ecclesiastical divisions as well as across the gulf of the centuries. There is, we shall maintain, a continuing community which is 'more than a bond of understanding and cooperation between its members; it is also a locus of transforming power making itself felt in the lives of its members and in the course of the complex affairs of the epoch in which it exists'. Such a community exists 'in virtue of its peculiar structure as a living unity of a one and a many'; [7] it exists as a unity in diversity, a diversity in unity, as the body of Christ living in the power of the Spirit.

II

In two previous books, *The World is a Wedding* and *The Kingdom of Love and Knowledge* I set out to explore aspects of this one Christian tradition, 'this living unity of a one and a many'. One of the underlying convictions in both books, everywhere assumed though not often explicitly affirmed, is that there is a substantial unity of prayer and life which has linked together men and women through the centuries of division in ways which are not always easily apparent. This unity of prayer and life is not divorced from faith and doctrine. It reflects a unity of faith in the one God, Father, Son and Holy Spirit, which has persisted underneath the questions of controversy and which has created bonds stronger than all the divisions which have been made within the Christian family. The use in those two earlier books of examples taken from the world of the continental Reformation and British Methodism as well as from the traditions of Anglicanism and Rome has been intended to show the breadth of this underlying unity. The central, and in some sense even normative, place given to the witness of Eastern Orthodoxy, a reality for too long ignored in the West, has also been of fundamental importance. Throughout I have presupposed an appeal to the witness of 'the undivided Church', the Church of the first ten centuries. In the unanimity of that first Christian age we can see the roots of the unity which has been maintained even through the schisms of the second millennium, the pledge and promise of the restoration of unity in the third millennium which is to come.

The term 'the undivided Church' however is not without its difficulties, historical and theological, and for that reason I have generally avoided its use. It is an expression which was dear to the leaders of the Oxford Movement, one hundred and fifty years ago. By it they declared their allegiance to the Church of the Fathers, and their conviction that despite all the outward separations, a real unity still existed between the communions of Constantinople, Canterbury and Rome. At that time their view was considered quixotic and unreal on almost every side. Protestants, naturally enough, ignored it since it ignored them. Both Constantinople and Rome wholly rejected it, for both claimed to be the whole Church in opposition to one another and in total exclusion of the world of the reformation. Both parties maintained that precisely because the Church must be one it is impossible to recognize the existence of divisions inside the Church. Each felt constrained to claim to be the whole. In recent years this situation has changed dramatically. For an Anglican there is something profoundly moving in the spectacle of a meeting between the Pope of Rome and the Patriarch of Constantinople, in which the heads of the two great Churches fully recognize one another, in which both look to the breaking down of the barriers which have divided them for hundreds of years, and in which both appeal explicitly to the witness of the 'undivided Church'. The vision which was born in Oxford in the 1830s, is now more widely spread throughout the Christian world. The conviction implicit throughout this book, as throughout its two predecessors, that the interpenetration of the separated Christian traditions is continuing and growing receives an almost unhoped for confirmation.

But this new and promising situation does not of itself remove the difficulty of speaking about the 'undivided Church'. Even if we use the phrase historically to speak of the Church of the first ten centuries, we have to recognize that it is, at best, only relatively true; true, that is, in comparison with the centuries which followed after. For already in the fifth century one of the fundamental splits in Christendom had taken place, that between the churches which accepted the decisions of the Council of Chalcedon, in 451, and those which did not. And at numerous times during those early centuries, other, less permanent controversies made divisions within the body of the Church. The unanimity of the witness of the Fathers is anything but uniform. It is always a unity in diversity. Was the Church, we may ask, *ever* undivided? At times we are tempted to say 'No'; but to do so is to fail to recognize the continuing communion between the greater part of the East and the West which marked the first ten centuries, that underlying coherence of faith and doctrine which was maintained for so long in spite of recurrent tensions and evident differences of emphasis and outlook. At least in this historical sense, as referring to the time before the great schism between the old and the new Rome, the term has its limited but real validity.

How far is it possible to use the term in a wider and more theological sense, to speak of that underlying unity of the Church which has been maintained through all the subsequent centuries of separation? Here the problems about its meaning multiply. The limitations of the view held by the leaders of the Oxford Movement become even more apparent. Their theory said nothing of the continuing life of the non-Chalcedonian Churches of the East, nothing of the continuing life of much the greater part of Protestantism. In itself it can only take us a certain way in our attempt to relate the opposed and contradictory realities with which Christians have to live, the fact of division on one side, the discovery of a God-given unity on the other. How, in face of these tensions, can we meaningfully speak of the one tradition?

In this book I have tried to grapple with this question by looking a little more at the way in which the Christian tradition operates in the life of prayer and faith, and in particular by looking at certain strands of that tradition as it has been received in the island of Britain, itself a larger and more variegated reality than is sometimes realized. In the second and third chapters, for instance, we examine two crucial moments in the development of that tradition in England and in Scotland, the second half of the fourteenth and the first half of the seventeenth centuries. In the fourth chapter we ask what light can be shed on our problem from some of the Celtic elements in our common tradition, which are often forgotten. In the fifth chapter we look at some of the less obvious implications of the recovery of a greater sense of unity amongst Christians during this century, and in particular at its relevance to the growing dialogue

15

between Christians and men of other faiths. In chapter six we consider directly some of the insights of T. S. Eliot which have been of importance throughout our discussion. And always the question of unity is considered not only as a contemporary problem but also as a question of unity in time, of the recovery of a living sense of the wholeness of tradition. If what is called 'ecumenism' today sometimes seems flat and superficial, it is in large part because the many dimensions of the question of unity are often ignored. Here we have tried to keep them in view.

The question with which we start then is the question of how the present is related to the past, how the Church of today can be the same Church as the Church of the apostles. If there is, as we shall argue, a real unity and co-inherence across the centuries, then perhaps we can speak of the undivided Church of the first milennium as providing the basis of a unity which has existed even through the centuries of separation. The one Church still lives and works within the separated Churches of the late twentieth century. It has never ceased to live in them. To say, as Christians too easily do, 'we are one in Christ', 'we are one in the Spirit', is to make assertions about the flesh and blood realities of history, since it is always in flesh and blood, not in some abstract realm, that men and women are called to live in Christ. As Eliot makes clear 'the point of intersection of the timeless with time' is necessarily particular and incarnate. We live as embodied creatures, part of a tradition and a community which exists 'in flesh and in Spirit'. In order to realize our unity with one another today, we need to recognize our unity with those who have preceded us. We need always to acknowledge that this unity is the gift of God, above all made known in faith, in prayer and in penitence. The new reality which was inaugurated on the day of Pentecost, the communion of men and women with one another within the very life of God, binds us together and has bound us together in ways we need further to explore. That is why questions about the meaning of prayer, both corporate and personal, are never far from the surface of our concern, and why the question of unity is always seen as rooted in its deepest dimension, the restoration of the union of man with God.

I have stressed in many places in this book that we seem at the present time to be in a new situation, a situation which enables us to perceive some things with a new and startling clarity. But we must not overestimate that element of newness. What is written here is itself the product of a tradition, the Anglican, one of whose most eminent spokesmen Thomas Ken, Bishop of Bath and Wells, could write at the beginning of the eighteenth century: 'As for my religion, I die in the Holy Catholic and Apostolic faith, professed by the whole Church before the disunion of East and West. . . .' and in his commentary on the Creed, Ken could pray 'O my God, amidst the deplorable divisions of thy Church, O let me never widen its breaches, but give me Catholic charity to all who are baptized in they name, and Catholic communion with all Christians in desire. O deliver me from the sins and errors, from the schisms and heresies of the age. O give me grace to pray daily for the peace of the Church and earnestly to seek it. . . .'[8] It is my hope that at least something of the spirit of that prayer has informed the pages that follow.

Chapter 1

The Presence of the Past

The subject which is before us, the presence of the past in the present, the dynamic of tradition, is of the utmost importance for all the world religions. All refer back either to some founding figure, or as in the case of Hinduism, to a group of ancient texts, which are granted primary sacred significance. For all of them this reference to the past is, in some degree, an embarrassment in the twentieth century. We live at a moment when our ways of thinking, acting and feeling are changing so rapidly that there is a tendency to believe that only what is turned towards the future can be of real importance. Though I shall be arguing throughout this book for the importance of remembering the past, our concern with it will not be antiquarian. We shall be dealing much with past history, but we shall always be concerned with it as it makes itself known to us in the present, and always as it makes it possible for us to live creatively towards the future. As Eliot remarks, 'Time present and time past/Are both perhaps present in time future.' One of the convictions which underlie these pages is that it is only as we gather up the past in its fulness now, that we can live with real freedom towards the time which is coming. We are not liberated from the past by forgetting it. Rather I would believe the reverse is true.

And if this subject is one which touches all the world's religions, it touches Christianity with a particular urgency. To be a Christian is to confess Jesus Christ as Lord and Saviour, and to do this involves recognizing the present authority and activity of one who lived nearly two thousand years ago. The person of Christ is central to Christian faith and life in a way which neither Mohammed nor

18

the Buddha is in their own traditions. The reference to the past is inescapable. Even those forms of Christianity which are least eager to speak about tradition as such, which seek to establish a direct contact between the believer and the text of the Bible, cannot avoid the problems of the relationship of the past to the present. It is inherent in the nature of the act of faith in Christ. As to those forms of Christianity which make much of ideas of the continuity of the Church's life and doctrine, which rejoice in the word tradition, they too are constantly meeting problems about its nature, about how it maintains itself and develops, about how we can distinguish true from false in its development.

This is particularly the case in Roman Catholic theology at the present time. The predominantly non-historical character of the official theology of the Roman Church before Vatican II has given way to an attitude more ready to recognize the variations of historical situation and perspective which have occurred in the course of the Church's history. But this reference to the past is not only a matter of doctrine and theology. At the heart of Christian prayer, as it is practised in the great majority of Christian traditions, there is a rite which we perform in obedience to a command: 'Do this *in remembrance* of me.' The words in the original Greek εἰς τὴν ἐμὴν ἀνάμνησιν are susceptible of various interpretations. But however they are interpreted, they are relevant to the theme we have chosen, and we shall hear of them again. Indeed the practice of Christian worship will give us clues which will be of crucial importance to us in our quest, for prayer has a curious way of altering our perspectives on time, being in itself an encounter between eternity and time, a moment in which the past is recalled and the future anticipated in an activity which sets in motion the deepest levels of the human psyche, levels which seem to be less closely tied to the sequence of time than is the conscious mind.

I

I want however to begin not with a Christian rite or doctrine, but with an essay of T. S. Eliot's published in 1919, that is to say almost ten years before he announced his adherence to Christian faith and practice, the essay entitled 'Tradition and the Individual Talent'. In it he speaks of the vital importance of tradition for the writer, and of the way in which past and present come together in any creative work. But before we come to this particular essay, it may be well to ask ourselves why Eliot should be so important for our enquiry. In the course of these pages we shall constantly be returning to his work, and we shall find that he is one who can tell us much on this subject of the relation of the past to the present, of this active presence of the past in our life today. Why should this be so? The answer is intimately bound up with the development of Eliot's own life. In the course of it he had made two notable and significant personal decisions. Born an American, growing up in St Louis on the banks of the Mississipi, conscious of the New England roots of his family, he transferred his life from one side of the Atlantic to the other, and, without renouncing his American upbringing, decided to make his home in the English tradition which lay behind the American world he had known hitherto. Hence we find in his work a particularly sharp awareness of what it is that characterizes the English tradition. Hence also that special interest in the seventeenth century, which he shares with many American scholars, the century which saw the conflicts in the Old England which gave birth to the New.

But having traced his origins back across the Atlantic, Eliot decided to make another and more radical return to the roots. Brought up as a Unitarian, he decided in adult life to accept the historic faith of the Church, faith in God as Trinity, faith in the incarnation of Jesus Christ, faith in the active presence of Christ in the sacraments, the extensions of the incarnation; having made that decision, he lived and thought through that faith with a consistency and a generosity not often seen in this century. With his formidable intelligence and his particular awareness as a writer, it is not surprising that he has important things to say to us. It is interesting to compare his understanding and experience of the faith with that of a great Anglican thinker of the nineteenth century, F. D. Maurice. Like Eliot, Maurice came from a Unitarian background; like him it was only as an adult that he decided to accept baptism into the name of the Trinity. In many ways very dissimilar, Eliot and Maurice are united by a common adherence to the Catholic faith as professed and taught in the Church of England, to what Ken had called 'the Holy Catholic and Apostolic faith professed by the whole Church before the disunion of East and West'. This is the inheritance they seek to enter into. To some extent also, both men share a common indebtedness to Coleridge, and as Stephen Prickett points out in his fine study, *Romanticism and Religion*, they have a similar attitude to the relation between national and universal in the Christian tradition, seeing them, not as opposed, but even as necessary to one another. 'National, for Maurice, is not the antithesis of universal; it is rather the necessary condition of universality. To belong to a universal society a man must have roots in one particular place. The man who is at home anywhere is at home nowhere. In embryo a Coleridgean position, this is an argument we find restated in the twentieth century by both T. S. Eliot and Simone Weil,' [1] and in Eliot's case, not only in theory but in life.

Eliot was, then, a man who had become English, entered the Church of England and become a Catholic Christian by mature decision. In both cases he is able to speak about the tradition he embraced in a way not easily accessible to those who have entered into it by birth and upbringing. Changes of nationality, like changes of church allegiance, can have a greater positive value than we are sometimes ready to admit, especially when they are made without any violent repudiation of the past. They can be ways of bringing together positions formerly thought to be incompatible, or at least unrelated, ways in which new insight can be gained into both sides of the barrier which has been crossed. As Pusey saw in a flash of prophetic vision in 1845, the conversion of his friend J. H. Newman from the Church of England to Rome need not in itself divide the churches; it could have the effect of bringing them together. Something of the largeness and inclusiveness of tradition may be glimpsed through such a movement.

It is clear then that Eliot himself was a man who from his own experience pondered deeply on the nature of tradition, on the relation of the past to the present. In the essay we are about to consider his concern is with the importance of literary tradition for the work of the poet, but his words have a relevance far beyond the immediate subject he was dealing with, and can apply equally well to tradition, considered in the life of the Church, and of the nations which are called into the Church. And here in this juxtaposition of Church and nation which we can hardly fail to make when we speak of T. S. Eliot, it is vital at the outset to make some clear distinctions. Church and nation are both vital vehicles of tradition, but they are never wholly identical. Even when, as has happened at times in the two thousand years of Christian history, they seem to coincide the distinction between them must be maintained. The nation is of this world, the Church, though called to be fully present in this world, is like its Lord not of this world. By its own nature it is called to be universal; it can never be confined to a single people, a single culture or a single civilization. It must always be crossing frontiers and breaking down barriers in the name of the Son of Man. But this universality does not mean that the Church can be indifferent or hostile to the local, the particular, the rooted. Quite the reverse is true. The universality of the Church, its true Catholicity, is never something uniform or abstract. It expresses itself through the multiplicity of peoples and languages, through all the multiplicity of human persons. It never, when it is true to itself, reduces this multiple diversity, which is an aspect of the God-given richness of creation, to a mere uniformity. It is in the diversity of the tongues that the unity of Pentecost is realized. This is a unity which is established by the creation of bonds of love and knowledge between those who are different; by an opening of hearts and minds to one another, in which each is confirmed in his God-given identity and character, and is at the same time enabled to respect and appreciate the gifts which are proper to the other, thus being enriched by them.

That these things are true at the level of personal relationships is something which is often readily acknowledged. The unifying work of Christ and the Holy Spirit is never something which destroys the true freedom, the true uniqueness of each human person. Rather it is in relationship with others, in deepening communion with them, that each one is enabled to become his unique self. But that this is also true, in some similar way, of nations and languages is less readily accepted. But here, I would maintain, there is a real analogy, and pressures towards uniformity are no less destructive. As Alexander Solzhenitsyn declared in his Nobel Prize speech, the languages and traditions of the human race are part of the irreplaceable richness of our human heritage. The language and literature even of a small people (were the people of Ancient Israel ever so numerous?) enshrines something irreplaceable in the experience of mankind. Here too the work of the Spirit can bring men together without making them all the same.

It has been part of the tragedy of Western Christendom since the sixteenth century, that this interpenetration of the Church and the nation has been only imperfectly perceived and lived. On the one side the Roman Catholic Church has tended towards policies which have made for an impersonal, authoritarian uniformity. On the other side the national churches which have developed in the Protestant world, have too often allowed themselves to be confined, imprisoned within the boundaries of a single nation, thereby losing their sense of the Church's nature as a universal communion of faith and life. One of the strongest attractions of the Eastern Orthodox tradition lies in its capacity to hold together within a single church family, peoples and cultures as diverse as the Greek, the Russian, the Romanian. It is a remarkable sign of life-giving convergence at the present time that in Pope John Paul II, the Roman Church should have a bishop with such a powerful conviction of the unique and God-given ways in which the one faith becomes rooted in the particular histories of particular peoples, who on this issue speaks with a distinctively Eastern Christian voice. His vivid awareness of the interpenetration of the universal and the particular in the history of his own nation, so movingly expressed in his speeches during his visit to Poland, is something which the Pope seems to want to apply to all the nations which he visits.

It is in the lives of the saints, those men and women in whom human life has begun to reach its fulfilment in God, who, in Eliot's words have received the calling 'to apprehend the point of intersection of the timeless with time' that we can see most clearly the nature of this interpenetration of the universal and the particular, of the heavenly and the earthly, of grace and nature. In the saints we see not only all the diversity of human personality, but also a kind of translucence of national identity, in the faces of men and women who, because they are free from the limitations and restrictions of what is particular, seem able, in that very freedom, to give a perfect expression to all that is of God in what they have inherited. In them, it is as though a whole people can become conscious of its own particular calling. Who could be more English than Julian of Norwich, Thomas More or Edward King? Who could be more Russian than Seraphim of Sarov, more Italian than Francis of Assisi? Each Christian nation could offer its own examples of men and women who sum up and fulfil a whole tradition of life and devotion. Just as *the* Incarnation took place within the history of a particular people, a particular place, a particular language, so too all lesser incarnations are to be found in particular times and places, cradled within particular ways of living and experiencing the intersection of the timeless with time. Hence whether we consider, England, Scotland or Russia, the fourteenth or the seventeenth century, it is always in the particular that the universal is revealed.

When we now turn to the essay of T. S. Eliot's to which we have already referred, we find that its discussion of tradition in relation to literature already implicitly raises many of these issues. Taken in itself the essay could be seen as a somewhat polemical plea for the recognition of the importance of tradition for the work of the writer. It clearly reflects Eliot's own situation in seeking to find and understand the roots of his own creative ability. Tradition, he maintains, is not something we can take for granted. 'It cannot be inherited, and if you want it you must obtain it by great labour. It involves, in the first place, the historical sense, which we may call nearly indispensable to anyone who would continue to be a poet beyond his twenty-fifth year; [Eliot was, when he wrote this, just past thirty] and *the historical sense involves a perception, not only of the pastness of the past, but of its presence*, the historical sense compels a man to write not only with his own generation in his bones, but with *a feeling that the whole literature of Europe from Homer until today, and within it the whole literature of his own country, has a simultaneous existence and composes a simultaneous order.* This historical sense which is *a sense of the timeless as well as the temporal and of the timeless and the temporal together*, is what makes a writer most acutely conscious of his place in time, of his own contemporaneity.' [2] In other words it is the sense of the past which makes us truly aware of the present, conscious of our own place in time, at least when the past is known as involving the timeless as well as the temporal, and is known as being in some way contemporary with us.

From this passage I would like to take three points, all at first sight somewhat paradoxical:

1. The 'historical sense' is said to imply not only a sense of the pastness of the past, but also of its presence.

2. The whole literature of a civilization, and within it the whole literature of a nation 'has a simultaneous existence and composes a simultaneous order'.

3. The historical sense implies a sense of 'the timeless and the temporal together', or as Eliot will say in his later writings a sense of 'the point of intersection of the timeless with time'. It seems that history is only to be known as history when it meets something greater than itself.

To these I will add a fourth and even more challenging assertion from the same essay. One who comes to think in this way 'will not find it preposterous that the past should be altered by the present, as much as the present is directed by the past. And the poet who is aware of this will be aware of great difficulties and responsibilities.' [3]

These are words of a very great poet who was also a distinguished literary critic, and they will play a central part in the course of our investigation. For the present I would like to suggest that they have an application far beyond the realm of literature. They are saying things which are important for understanding human existence in general, and particularly important for understanding whatever Christian existence may be. They suggest forcibly that Eric Gill, the sculptor and writer, was right when he maintained that it is not the artist who is a particular kind of man, but that every man is a particular kind of artist. The acquisition of an historical sense, which Eliot says is necessary to every poet who wishes to continue to be a poet after his twenty-fifth year, is I believe necessary to everyone who would wish to continue to be a human being as he grows older. Of course we shall have to enlarge the meaning of the words 'historical sense', so that they signify at least some awareness of one's own life as being a story with a meaning, some sense however rudimentary of a personal history, and in some perhaps unformulated way, a sense of that personal history being linked with the story of one's tribe, one's people, one's Church, perhaps even of humanity. Without some such awareness of history, it is difficult for any sense of personal identity to survive. Without some such ability to remember that past, it becomes all but impossible to face the future with hope and a sense of purpose.

John Macquarrie in his *Principles of Christian Theology* gives a remarkably clear account of this threefold pattern as it affects our personal existence.

> What constitutes existence or personal being is a peculiar and complex temporal nexus in which the three dimensions of past, present and future are brought into a unity. Man differs from a thing or even from an animal in so far as he is not only aware of the present but remembers the past and anticipates the future. The basically temporal structure of existence was deeply understood by St Augustine, who says of the mind that, 'It both expects and considers and remembers.' This is the 'moment' of which existentialist philosophers from Kierkegaard to Heidegger have written, the authentic present that does not shut out either past or future, but, through openness to both, forges them into unity. In an existence that is scattered and disrupted, the existent has cut himself off from one or other of the temporal dimensions of existence, . . . On the other hand, in an existence that is fulfilling its potentialities, the three dimensions are held together in unity. Their balance and tension are maintained.[4]

What is said here of the life of the individual would be no less true of the life of a human community.

It may be said that to speak in this general sense of the necessity for a sense of the past in the present is to enlarge Eliot's meaning illegitimately. But as we have already suggested his words have a remarkably rich potential of meaning. We know that he was delighted when readers discovered in his poetry meanings of which he had not been consciously aware. Perhaps we shall find that the same thing is true, in a measure, of his prose. These are ideas we shall be exploring later in this book. For the present I propose to pursue this theme of our personal past as linked with larger and more universal acts of remembering, and as present within us not merely by way of nostalgia and reminiscence, by taking the rather perilous path of recalling certain moments of my own past, not particularly spectacular or scandalous ones, but moments which have remained a living part of myself for more than a quarter of a century, and which have, among other things, greatly illumined my reading of that passage from Eliot.

The year is 1955, the month October, the place a monastery on one of the Greek islands. The monastery was famous neither for its architecture nor for its history; it had been founded little more than a century before. It was however well known for the quality of its life and for the character of its abbot, at that time one of the three or four best known spiritual fathers (*gerontes*) in the Church of Greece. The visit there was a memorable one for me in many ways. It was for instance my first experience of a life not dominated by clocks and wirelesses. The style of life was very much that of the preindustrial Greek countryside. The majority of the monks were themselves villagers; there was only one amongst them who spoke any language other than Greek. The Abbot himself had a large old pocket watch which he would consult from time to time, and there was an impressive grandfather clock which ticked away in the Church. Apart from them there may not have been more than one or two other time pieces in the whole monastery, and if there were, they were kept in their place. When I asked what time Vespers would be I was told it would be when the fathers returned from the fields; when I asked what time the Night Office would begin I was told it would be when the bell rang. I do not mean to suggest that the life was irregular or disorderly. It had quite a strict though flexible rhythm to it, but it worked on human time rather than clock time. And if there was flexibility as well as strictness in the timetable, so though the style of life was austere, there was an extraordinary warmth and gentleness in the welcome given to this young foreigner.

But to come to our subject. The office of Mattins in a Greek monastery, as in many Western monasteries, begins at about three o'clock in the morning. In the Byzantine rite however it begins with six invariable psalms, one of which is always Psalm 63. In the darkened church with one or two lamps burning before the icon-ostasis the Abbot would recite the six psalms. ὁ Θεὸς ὁ Θεὸς μου πρὸς σε ὀρθρίζω: O God, thou art my God; early will I seek thee. My soul thirsteth for thee, my flesh also longeth after thee: in a barren and dry land where no water is.' [5] I said the Abbot would recite the psalms. But that gives the wrong impression. He spoke them as if they were being spoken for the first time, speaking them from the depths of his heart; and yet at the same time speaking them with the weight of almost three thousand years, a hundred generations of longing after God. It was as if the whole tradition was speaking through him. Scripture comes to fulfilment when it ceases to be scripture and becomes living speech. The Spirit who breathed in the original psalmist breathed in the man who now spoke the psalmist's words. They were words filled with the Spirit. One saw very clearly something about the presence of the past, about the self-renewing nature of tradition.

One day the Abbot took me to see the monastery library. It was not a very large collection of books. There were a lot of elderly, well-used volumes of the Fathers. 'Here' said the abbot, 'is a book which you give to beginners.' 'This is a work which is useful for someone who is depressed.' 'Here is a book which will give very clear instructions about the Jesus Prayer.' Any Westerner showing you round this collection of books, even someone to whom they were of practical use, would have said: 'Here is an interesting sixth century text.' 'This writer shows influences from the Syrian tradition,' 'Here is a work important in the later development of Hesychasm.' We look at books chronologically and classify them in terms of influences and development. To the Abbot they all had a simultaneous existence and composed a simultaneous order. They were all books which were useful for life in the Spirit. Their authors were fathers and teachers who had become friends, to whom one spoke in church and at other times; it was of little importance whether they had lived six hundred, twelve hundred or fifty years ago. He showed me the library rather in the way in which an expert gardener might show you his collection of books on gardening, or a cook a collection of cookery books. These help you on your way. They are not an end in themselves.

The impression gained in the library was re-inforced in the church. In the night office, for a major feast, the Abbot read part of a patristic homily expounding the mystery of the entry of the Mother of God into the Temple. The reading over, he shut the book and continued, in his own words but in precisely the same style, to unfold the mystery. Always in Orthodox worship, one has the impression that the books are being used as prompt books. When you can leave them aside you do. Then you just speak or sing from the heart. The word of God is a living word. The sense of contemporaneity with the past is sometimes very strong. The moment of prayer which is always a moment in which 'the timeless and the temporal' are held together reveals a surprising capacity for transcending the divisions of the centuries.

But now I must recount another slightly more complicated incident. One day I was sitting in my room reading. I was at that somewhat euphoric moment when one suddenly begins to discover that one can read another language fairly fluently. I was reading an account written by the abbot of a visit he had made as a young man to St Nektarios of Aegina, the most recently canonized of Greek saints. At that time – it must have been about the end of the first world war – the saint was living in retirement near a convent of nuns he had founded on the island of Aegina. The young man came to the convent and found an old workman digging in the fields outside the gate. He asked whether the Bishop Nektarios was there. The old man said, Yes, he would go and fetch him. A few minutes later, having tidied himself up and put on his cassock, the old man came back. He was the Bishop. Reading the story it struck me how similar it was to an incident in the life of the fourteenth century Russian abbot, St Sergius of Radonezh, who again was not recognized on account of the menial work he was doing. There is a kind of incognito of the saints; the man of God is often not recognized at first. And while all these thoughts were going through my mind a monk knocked at the door and asked if I would like to go for a walk. I replied, I hope fairly politely, that I was interested in what I was reading. A little while later he came back with the same suggestion. I suddenly realized that it was the abbot I had refused.

Reading an incident in the life of one saint had reminded me of an incident in the life of another, and had involved me directly in a tiny incident of precisely the same kind. I myself had unintentionally become part of the tradition. It struck me forcibly there and then, and not on subsequent reflection, that if very similar incidents occur in the lives of the saints, it is not always because monastic writers copy from one life to another. Certainly that sometimes happens. But people of a certain kind who live a certain style of life are likely to attract to themselves certain happenings, certain sayings, certain situations. The life of tradition renews itself constantly from within. We may sometimes make mistakes looking for literary dependence from one age to another, when in fact what we are seeing is the recurrence of a living pattern of words and actions.

To move from the trivial to something of infinitely greater significance. I do not for a moment suppose that St Francis of Assisi was aware of the incident in the life of the sixth century Breton saint, St Guenolé, in which the saint kisses a man with a particularly hideous leprosy and the leper turns into Christ. But the moment at which Francis overcame his physical repulsion for the lepers was one of the turning points of his life and it is one of the best attested facts in his story. He himself says in his Testament: 'When I was in sin, the sight of lepers nauseated me beyond measure; but then God himself led me into their company, and I had pity on them. When I had once become acquainted with them, what had previously nauseated me became a source of spiritual and physical consolation for me.' [6] It is a saying which throws much light back on to whatever incident it was that lies behind the story in the life of St Guenolé. Again though it is possible that he knew the life of St Francis, it does not seem likely that this story was in the mind of the volunteer from New York working in Mother Teresa's hospice for the dying in Calcutta who said that when he overcame his repulsion for touching the bodies of those dying of hunger and malnutrition he found that he was touching Christ. Rather we may see here the reality behind the story which is known in many lands, of an appalling horror which needs to be embraced to be transformed. We can also perhaps perceive something of the power of life in the words of Jesus when he assures his disciples that acts of kindness done to the least of their fellow-men are in fact done to him. These are words of one time which prove to be words for many times.

We have already begun to see that the passage of T. S. Eliot on the nature of tradition which we quoted at the beginning has Christian resonances of which he can hardly have been conscious at the time when he wrote it. It is frequently said that Christianity is par excellence an historical religion, in the sense both that it gives the greatest importance to the facts of history and is itself inescapably linked with historical events. This is indeed true, though not in the way in which it is sometimes taken, in which history is seen merely in terms of the chronological sequence of time. It is, I believe, only if we take the word historical in the sense in which Eliot uses it, as something which implies 'the time-less and the temporal together' that it is true to say that Christianity is a historical religion. Then, as we come to recognize the presence as well as the pastness of the past, the nearness of eternity to time, we shall find the present to be part of a larger 'simultaneous order' of which the past is also part.

We have already seen how this may become evident in the context of Christian prayer, have seen for instance how the words of the psalms, which for two thousand years have been the staple of Christian worship, express this with particular clarity. Built into Christian worship there is a way of holding together three different moments in time, the time of the Old Testament from which the words come, the time of Jesus through which they are interpreted and in which they were fulfilled, and the present time in which they are being used. There is a cumulative process of enrichment. The meaning of the scriptures is only gradually revealed in its fulness. We looked for a moment at Psalm 63, a psalm of personal devotion, hearing it recited by a single voice. But we could find the same thing even more clearly in the psalms which speak of the experience of the whole people of Israel. When, as is the usual practice in a Western monastery, the psalms are recited or sung by the whole community together, this corporate aspect of their meaning becomes powerfully evident. In such a use of the psalms we find an expression of the life of a whole people through the centuries of its history, an experience which is read through the prism of the things concerning Jesus, and then read again in the light of the historical experience of the Church. Here is a gathering of experience through the ages, a linking together of different and distinct times within a single act of affirmation and praise which joins what is temporal with what is more than temporal. And this pattern can have its own internal complexities and enrichments.

Let us take as an example, Psalm 107, one of the psalms which is full of the historical memories of Israel, and listen to it as it is used in Christian worship today, as used indeed in the daily round of worship in a monastery in Northern France. The people of Israel now established in the land of promise recall God's actions in the past which have brought them through the perils of the desert and the sea and created for them a city, a society in which men can

31

dwell together in peace. They give thanks for what God has done, and for what he now does, recalling how their fathers 'cried unto the Lord in their trouble and he delivered them from their distress. He led them forth by the right way, that they might go to a city where they dwelt. . . . O that men would praise the Lord for his goodness and declare the wonders that he doeth for the children of men.' [7] This double refrain occurs four times in the first part of the poem. The whole constitutes an act of thanksgiving to God who gives men the possibility of living together in community, of planting and building, of sowing and reaping, gathering together from East and West, from North and South into a settled community.

All this is not done without the effort and achievement of man, without anxiety and failure, without planning and vision. It is human life and history which we celebrate here, and that life and history is something which is not destroyed but fulfilled when the acts of God become manifest in time. For man was made for fellowship with God, and it is when he acts in co-operation with God that his acts become most truly human.

But now we are using these words two and a half millennia later. We have the accumulated experience of the Church behind us, the Church which from the beginning has seen itself called to be a universal community, in which men and women of all ages and places can find their place. And let us suppose that it happens that we are singing this psalm on the feast of St Cyril and St Methodius, the apostles of the Slavs. Here are additional layers of reminiscence, conscious and unconscious entering into the action. We think of the work of the two Greek missionaries who in the ninth century invented the Cyrillic alphabet in order to translate the Gospels, the Epistles, these very psalms and eventually the whole Bible into the Slavonic language. Along with the Scriptures the whole treasury of Byzantine liturgy was also translated, thereby laying the foundation of that fervent tradition of worship which has so deeply marked the history of the Russian people, and which still today after sixty years of atheist persecution and pressure has not been silenced. It is a tradition whose echoes we can hear in the poetry of Pasternak and in the prose of Solzhenitsyn. Indeed, the whole development of Eastern European culture, with all that it involves of human greatness and tragedy, has been marked for ever by the work of these two men.

Thus the Old Testament element in the psalm which had already referred us to different periods in the life of the people of Israel is fulfilled in the commemoration of two saints whose lives bring to mind a variety of periods in the history of the Church. There is an accumulation of memories from different ages. And these saints were translators, men whose work involved that transposition from one culture to another, that crossing of frontiers which is a necessary part of the preaching of the Gospel and in which we see something of the dynamic of tradition. We may well think of the amazing way in which that work of translation has gone forward in the last two centuries. It has often been Christian missionaries who have first reduced languages to writing in Asia, in Africa, in the Pacific so that these very same Scriptures might be made known, and so that all the peoples of the earth might be gathered in from East and West, from South and North, to this communion of life together. All this explicitly or implicitly is being made known in the use of the psalter in the worship of this particular monastery in France, on this particular day in February 1979.

It is important to note that the office to which we have just referred was celebrated not in Latin but in French, that is to say in forms of words and music which have been developed over the last twenty years. In that sense it was a very twentieth century act of worship, the product of a work of translation which is still in progress, throughout the Roman Catholic world. The traditional power of the liturgy does not depend on the preservation of particular verbal and musical formulas, however valuable and precious they may be. Rather it may be strengthened by movements of liturgical renewal and reform, when they are based on a sound grasp of liturgical principles, for such movements can release new powers of translation and interpretation. To think that the preservation of Latin with its accompanying chant, or, in the Anglican context, of the English of the sixteenth century, will of itself maintain the tradition, is to misconceive the nature of the operation which we are engaged in. David Jones, who perhaps more than any other writer of our century in England penetrated into the nature of tradition, insists that one of the essential qualities of a living work of art is its 'nowness'. True, it must be a 'transubstantiated

33

nowness', a contemporaneity which is transformed and fulfilled by the presence of the past and by the nearness of eternity, but this in no way absolves the work from the necessity of being of its own time and place. Eliot certainly saw this no less than David Jones. What is true of every work of art, is at least in some measure true of the liturgy itself. When it belongs most truly to its own time and place, it can, paradoxically, most truly convey truths and powers from other times and places, indeed from beyond all time and place. To put the matter in terms of current Anglican controversy, the revised rites which employ the English of the twentieth century, if intelligently used, are more capable of conveying the life of tradition than the familiar forms of the Prayer Books of the sixteenth and seventeenth century.

To enter into this worship is to become conscious, with varying degrees of awareness, of the literature of a whole people 'which has a simultaneous existence and composes a simultaneous order'. But it is not one which is static and fixed. As the Orthodox theologian, Andrei Scrima writes: 'it is not a question of a hidden continuation of a sacred past which would deny the temporal, but of a continuity of Presence, which is creative and life-giving at every moment – one could say of a contemporaneity of the Spirit'.[8] Christian worship is a celebration of the deeds of God, but deeds in which men are called to have their full share, the celebration of an order which is still growing and dynamic, to which we ourselves are contributing, of which we are a part. These are deeds which are done in time, but into which eternity enters, deeds by which time is gathered up into eternity, through the working together of the freedom of man and the life-giving Spirit of God. They are deeds marked by all the diversity and richness of man's development in the various periods of human history. The promise of Jesus to his disciples to send the Holy Spirit, translated in many English versions by the words, 'I will not leave you comfortless', in Latin reads *'Non vos relinquam orphanos'*,[9] I will not leave you orphans. By the activity of the Spirit Christ makes us all to be one family in God our Father. The barriers of time no less than the barriers of space are broken down. The diversity of times and nations is not destroyed, it is fulfilled in an hitherto unsuspected unity.

All this is declared with vividness in the life and worship of a monastic community, that is to say a group of men or women who have chosen to give the greater part of their time and energy to the work of prayer. It is not of course exclusively to be seen there. All Christian worship involves this recalling of the past through the use of the Scriptures. And at the heart of this worship there is always the rite which we perform in remembrance of Christ, for the forgiveness of sins. Indeed wherever Christian people experience 'the timeless and the temporal together', in the meeting of man with God, there the same reality is to be found. It can make itself known in innumerable places, and often in the most unlikely ones. At the heart of this experience there is always the fact of forgiveness, pardon, that paradoxical power of God to transform evil into good, and to bring life out of death, which makes it possible not to 'find it preposterous that the past should be altered by the present, as much as the present is directed by the past', which frees us from bondage to the past, so that we may live towards the future. Of this we shall speak further in a later chapter. Let it suffice to say at present that when the Byzantine writer Niketas Stethatos declares that 'tears of repentance may restore lost virginity' he is giving us a picture of Christianity very different from that commonly accepted in our English-speaking world, which has suggested that from the point of view of the Christian religion sexual sins are as unforgiveable as they are irreparable. He is telling us how, in Christian faith, it is believed that the moment of the intersection of the timeless and time, the moment when the eternal power of divine forgiveness and new life enters into the very heart of man, is a moment of such power that it can have effects backwards as well as forwards in time, turning the experience of loss into a new and deeper discovery of integrity.

Chapter 2

'Brethren of One Blood'

The views about tradition which Eliot expressed so forcefully in 'Tradition and the Individual Talent', were by no means merely theoretical. Rather they informed his own poetic work and became more clearly evident through the passage of the years. By the time we came to his last poetic work, *Four Quartets*, the theological implications of the position taken up in 1919 have become much more explicit. In these poems we have an extended meditation on the presence of the past, known and experienced as a moment in which temporal and timeless come together and are at one. The first of the *Quartets*, *Burnt Norton*, begins with the words:

Time present and time past
Are both perhaps present in time future . . .

As the poems go on it becomes clear that all moments of annunciation are seen to be linked with the one Annunciation; all moments of the 'intersection of the timeless with time', however fleetingly glimpsed are recognized as having the quality of incarnation in them, and are linked with the one Incarnation.

In the last of the *Quartets*, *Little Gidding*, Eliot powerfully evokes two moments in the history of England, moments of great importance to himself, moments of great importance to the English tradition as a whole, the second half of the fourteenth century and the first half of the seventeenth. They are times of a kind of flowering both intellectual and spiritual, times which have a lasting significance. Such times occur in the history of all nations and continue to be a source of strength and encouragement long after

36

they are over. In the case of England, because the English language has become the possession of many peoples beyond the island of Britain, these moments may have a wider significance. They are potentially part of the heritage of men and women in many different parts of the globe.

In this chapter we shall be looking at the fourteenth century, and in the subsequent one the seventeenth. But before we come to look at the two medieval writers to whom Eliot directly refers, it may be well to consider briefly the achievement of this period as a whole, the years between 1350 and 1400.

It was very far from being a period of untroubled calm. It knew the periodic devastations of a violent plague, the black death; it was marked by the savagery of the Peasant's Revolt and its still more savage repression. Yet in this half-century something wonderful happened in terms of the language and the literature of England. First the language itself emerged in a form in many ways still recognizable today, and became the language of the court as well as of the people, thus healing the linguistic division which had existed for three centuries in English society. Then it emerged in all its vigour and freshness, and was employed by a group of writers who may rightly stand comparison with the greatest of their successors. As so often happens the beginnings of a literary tradition are marked by a flowering of unusual quality.

One of the special characteristics of this half-century is that it saw the conjunction of a group of mystical writers whose work has never since been excelled in English, Julian, Walter Hilton, the author of *The Cloud*, and a little earlier Richard Rolle, with three outstanding poets, each very different from the other, but each marked, in his own particular way, by the profoundly Christian character of the age in which he lived, Chaucer, Langland and the Gawayne poet. The astonishing maturity and variety of Chaucer's art has always been recognized. Only more recently has there been such general recognition of the subtlety and genius, which mark the works of the unknown writer of *Gawayne and the Green Knight*. Because he used a dialect and a literary form which is unfamiliar to us, his work is generally less easily accessible. When we turn to Langland the case is different. The extraordinary range of feeling and understanding to be found in *Piers Plowman* has long been acknowledged in theory. In practice, however, has the central place of the work within the English religious tradition been properly realized? But in all these writers, whether in Julian or *The Cloud* or Walter Hilton, whether in Chaucer or Langland or *Gawayn* we are conscious that throughout English voices are speaking, voices which have the excellencies and the limitations which have marked the English tradition ever since, and that something of abiding significance is being said.

Eliot was concerned with this period from many points of view. He introduced it into the last of the *Four Quartets*, as he himself explains, partly in order to add greater historical depth to the poem, partly to balance what he feared might be too exclusive a concentration on the seventeenth century background. He brought it in by way of two brief but highly charged quotations, The first, 'With the drawing of this love and the voice of this calling,' is taken from *The Cloud of Unknowing*, The second 'Sin is behovely, but all shall be well, and all shall be well, and all manner of thing shall be well' from Julian of Norwich. When we turn to examine the work of these two writers, Julian and the author of *The Cloud*, we find ourselves in the presence of writers of a classical stature whose work can rightly be placed alongside the greatest products of the Christian mystical tradition. Neither, it is true, is systematic and all inclusive in their approach. But both show a depth of insight and a sureness of judgement which make it not inappropriate to speak of them in company with the classical figures of Christian East and West, with a Gregory of Nyssa on one side, or a John of the Cross on the other. Both write at that point of understanding where the distinction between mystic and theologian becomes no longer applicable, where there is a union of heart and mind, in a fulness of apprehension of the divine. I quote Thomas Merton on this point in relation to Julian of Norwich: 'She is a true theologian with greater clarity, depth and order than St Theresa: she really elaborates, theologically, the content of her revelations. She first experienced, then thought, and the thoughtful deepening of experience worked itself back into her life, deeper and deeper, until her whole life as a recluse at Norwich was simply a matter of getting completely saturated in the light she had received all at once, in the 'shewings', when she thought she was about to die.' [1] The moments of intense visionary experience which she knew in

38

her thirtieth year, were to live and grow in her for the rest of her life.

In terms of the relevance of the past to the present both writers have never been so widely read as within the last twenty years. In the case of Julian we have already seen how interest in her work has developed with striking rapidity. As to *The Cloud of Unknowing*, its popularity in our century has become even greater; the translation in the Penguin Classics has been reprinted eight times in the last ten years. It almost seems as if these writers of the fourteenth century had had in mind the situation of the late twentieth century. It is clear that they can speak to our condition.

But what is no less important is that both, in their very different ways, are themselves the products of tradition. This is most evident in the case of the author of *The Cloud*, who expresses, in an accessible and balanced form, the way of approach to God which proceeds by way of the recognition that nothing that we say or think or imagine about him can equal the one whom we approach. He follows in the line of one of the most influential of all the writers of Greek patristic theology, the fifth century Syrian monk who goes by the name of Dionysius the Areopagite. Indeed he made a rather free translation of the shortest but most important of all the works of Dionysius, *The Mystical Theology*, or as it becomes in middle English, *Dionise Hid Divinite*. The negative or apophatic theological way, still central to the tradition of Eastern Christianity, is thus made accessible to the ordinary reader of English, by way of the author of *The Cloud of Unknowing*. It is curious to reflect that Dionysius is in process of becoming the best known of the Greek Fathers in the English-speaking world.

With Mother Julian, the links to the earlier tradition are less easy to see. It has been the custom to read her against the background of the scholastic theology which was developing in her own day; the results were unsatisfactory and puzzling, for she will not fit into this kind of framework. But in the most recent detailed studies of her work it has become clear that she too needs to be read against the background of the Bible and the earlier tradition to be truly appreciated.[2] It is in relation to the teaching of the Fathers and in particular the Eastern Fathers that one of the most important and controversial parts of her teaching, her view of the end of all things, is best to be understood. It is this which particularly attracted Eliot. Julian maintains in tension the faith of the Church, itself based on many sayings in the Gospels, that at the final judgement there will be a separation of good from evil, with the showing that she herself has received that at the last day 'all shall be well and all shall be well, and all manner of thing shall be well'. How this can be she does not know. That at that day it will be so, that the Holy Trinity will do 'a great deed' she is assured. She refuses to fall into the heresy on the one side, of teaching an automatic universalism which denies the reality of judgement, but on the other side she refuses to fall into that other way of seeing things which for long prevailed in the West, which stresses the reality of judgement in such a way as to deny the very possibility of hope that all shall be well. I quote Thomas Merton again: 'This is, for her, is the heart of theology: not solving the contradiction but remaining in the midst of it, in peace, knowing that it is fully solved, but that the solution is secret, and will never be guessed until it is revealed.' [3]

The apparent optimism of Julian is very far from being the optimism of one who refuses to see the suffering and evil in the world. Her own experience begins with a vision of Christ on the cross, of a frightening intensity. She says at one place; 'We see deeds done that are so evil, and injuries inflicted that are so great, that it seems to us quite impossible that any good can come of them.' [4] Who in the age of Belsen and the Gulag Archipelago can say otherwise? She refuses to speculate as to the origins of evil, but she sees that it is there. In the words which Eliot quotes, she understands that 'Sin is behovely; but all shall be well, and all shall be well and all manner of thing shall be well'. And she goes on 'In this simple word *sin* our Lord reminded me in a general sort of way of all that is not good; the despicable shame and utter self-denial he endured for us, both in his life and in his dying. And of all the suffering and pain of his creatures, both spiritual and physical. . . . All this I saw, together with all the suffering that ever has been or can be. [O brave and valiant woman] . . . . All this was shown in a flash, and quickly passed over into consolation – for our good Lord would not have the soul frightened by this ugly sight.' [5] If she believes in the triumph of good, it is a good which can triumph through suffering and pain, which can redeem all that is evil. She affirms with her own simplicity and balance the Christian faith not only that through God's forgiveness the past can be altered by the present, but that by a supreme act of creative love, God in the end will show that all that is passed can be altered, and all things brought to fulfilment in him.

It is very evident that this question of the salvation of all, was one which at this time pressed hard upon others as well as the mystics. We shall find the poets concerned with it too. In particular we shall find them troubled by the question about the salvation of those who came before Christ. The Christian tradition has in general held that baptism and faith in Christ are necessary to man's eternal salvation. It was this faith which amongst other things motivated the extraordinary missionary efforts of all the churches in the last two centuries. But what of those who lived before Christ? What of those who had no chance of baptism? Can the effects of Christ's incarnation run backwards as well as forwards in time? The question pressed heavily on the medieval believer, and it forms the subject of a little known but wonderful poem from the period we are considering, *St Erkenwald*.[6]

The first thing to note about the poem, is the acute sense of time which it evinces. It begins:

At London in Englond noght long sythen,
Sythen Christ suffrid on Crosse and Christendom stablid . . .

(At London in England, not so very long after
Christ suffered on the cross and established Christendom . . .)[7]

It is a poem written in the fourteenth century, about a bishop (the fourth bishop of London) who lived seven hundred years earlier, and it is concerned with a figure who had lived over a thousand years earlier than that. The many layered pattern of periods which the Christian way of interpreting the Old Testament by means of the New made familiar, is here seen at work. But if the poem shows an acute sense of time, it shows a no less vivid sense of place. It is centred on St Paul's Cathedral, itself described as the place where all the city comes together.

There commen thider of all kynnes so kenely many
That as all the worlde were thider walon wytin a hondequile.

(So many of all kinds, were keen to be there

41

that all the world seemed to have turned out at once.)[8]

At the time when the poem was written extensive re-building was going on in the Cathedral. Something of this is reflected in the description of the seventh-century construction of the Cathedral as the poet imagines it. Then too there was building, or rather re-building going on, for, as he explains to us, the Cathedral was constructed on the site of an ancient pre-Christian temple. There is layer upon layer of history. As they dig deep into the foundations they find a great tomb embellished with marble, with an inscription which no one can read. They open it and find within an uncorrupt body, splendidly dressed in velvet and ermine, a crown on the head and a sceptre in the hand. What can be the meaning of this marvel? Who is this royal figure? No one can tell. They send to summon the bishop who is on a visitation in Essex. He returns to the capital, passes through the crowds who throng around him, shuts himself into his palace and spends the night in prayer.

And so long he grette after grace that he graunte hade
An answare of the Holy Goste, and afterwards hit dawid.

(So long did he plead for grace that it was granted,
An answer from the Holy Ghost; dawn came after that.)[9]

The Bishop goes into church, celebrates a Mass of the Holy Spirit, and then accompanied by the mayor and notables of the city comes to the tomb.

There follows a long exchange between the Bishop and the dead man. No, he replies, he was not himself king; he was chief justice in this city many years before Christ. He had ruled a fractious and difficult people, but always with justice and equity. That is why at the time of his death he was buried with royal honours. But where now, the Bishop asks, is your soul; how does it come that your body lies here uncorrupt?

Then hummyd he that ther lay and his hedde waggyd
And gife a gronyng ful grete and to Godde sayde,
Mighty maker of men, thi myghtes are grete
How myght thi mercy to me amounte any tyme?
Nas I a paynym unpreste that never thi plite knewe,
Ne thi misure of thi mercy ne thi mecal vertue?

(The man lying there murmured and moved his head,
And gave a great groan, and said to God:
'Strong Maker of men, great is thy might.
How could thy mercy come at any time to me?
Was I not a dull pagan who never knew thy pledge,
Nor the measure of thy mercy, nor thy mighty power. . . .')[10]

As he explains how his soul remains in darkness, shut out from the feast of God's eternal kingdom, the Bishop weeps, and as he weeps a tear falls onto the face of the corpse, and as it does so the corpse dissolves. The soul is released and received into heavenly joy.

Then was lovyng oure Lorde wyt loves uphalden
Meche mournyng and myrthe was mellyd togeder.
Thai passyd forth in processiun and all the pepull followid
And all the belles in the burghe beryd at ones.

(Then praise to our Lord rose from uplifted hands;
much mourning and mirth were intermingled.
They passed forth in procession, the people followed
while all the bells in the town boomed out together.)[11]

The invention of the poem is surely superb. We see London, the place since at least Roman times associated with the sovereignty of the southern part of this island, the *unbeniaeth Prydain* as the Welsh tradition calls it; at its heart St Paul's Cathedral, and deep within the church, the buried, ancestral figure. The Bishop comes, seeking divine guidance, filled with the Holy Spirit, his heart and mind overflowing in tears of compassion. Early theologians seeking to mitigate the rigour of the teaching about the necessity of baptism for salvation had spoken of a baptism of blood in the case of the martyrs who had died for the faith before they could be baptized. Others had spoken of a baptism of desire, a baptism conferred by the longing after that which was not outwardly received. Here the desire of the judge is met by the compassion of the Bishop and there is a baptism of tears. We are reminded of the power attributed to tears of repentance in the Eastern Fathers, tears which are called a second baptism and sometimes said to be stronger than baptism itself. We see again how through the grace of God meeting the desire and work of man, even the past can be changed by the

43

present. As Eliot will say 'Here past and future/Are conquered and reconciled'. And all this is found at the heart of the city, the particular city in which Eliot lived and worked and wrote his poetry.

This same problem of the salvation of the righteous pagan, is treated again in what is arguably the greatest single poem of this period, *Piers Plowman*. I say 'arguably' because I do not wish to affirm that it is a greater poem than either *Troilus and Criseyde* or *The Canterbury Tales*. In assurance and maturity of style, in depth and width of human feeling, Chaucer is so great a master, that in some ways Langland can hardly be compared with him. Yet there are things that Langland knew that Chaucer did not know. He knows and can speak of the plight of the poor in a medieval city in a way that no one else, except perhaps Villon, can do. When he speaks about the bitterness of poverty he knows what he is talking about. At the same time he can enter into and give voice to the central mysteries of Christianity in a way equalled by few poets in English before or since. As David Jones remarks he is at once more earthy and more celestial than his great contemporary. Consider these lines on the incarnation.

> For Truthe telleth that love is triacle of hevene:
> May no synne be on hym seene that that spice useth.
> For hevene myghte nat holden it, so was it hevy of hymself,
> Till it hadde of the erthe eten his fille.
> And whan it hadde of this fold flessh and blood taken,
> Was never leef upon lynde lighter therafter,
> And portatif and persaunt as the point of a nedle,
> That myghte noon armure it lette ne none heighe walles.
> Forthi is love ledere of the Lordes folke of hevene. . . .

(Love is Heavens sovereign remedy, and he who takes it has no trace of sin left . . . Heaven could not hold love, it was so heavy in itself. But when it had eaten its fill of earth, and taken flesh and blood, then it was lighter than a leaf on a linden-tree, more subtle and piercing than the point of a needle. The strongest armour was not proof against it, the tallest ramparts could not keep it out.
Therefore Love is first among the company of the Lord of Heaven.)[12]

44

There is here a very remarkable use of language, an incomparable example of the 'translucence' of the universal in the particular, which Coleridge declares to be of the nature of true symbolism. It is a quality also to be found in some of the anonymous religious lyrics of this same period, perhaps made possible by the newness of the language and the depth of faith of a whole people. It occurs in many places in Langland.

In Passus XI, there is a passage which deals with the legend of the Roman Emperor Trajan, who it was believed had been released from hell at the prayers of Pope Gregory the Great. As often happens in Langland, there is at this point a sudden intervention of a new voice into the narrative.

'Ye, baw for bokes!' quod oon was broken out of helle.
'I Troianus, a trewe knyght, take witnesse at a pope
How I was ded and dampned to dwellen in pyne
For an uncristene creature; clerkes wite the sothe –
That all the clergie under Criste ne mythte me cracche fro helle
But oonliche love and leautee and my laweful domes.'

(Bah! Who cares about books!' said a man called Trajan, who had once been a true knight, and had broken loose from Hell. And now he swore, on the word of a Pope, that he had once been dead and damned for being a pagan. – 'The fact is well known among scholars', he said. 'Not all the learning of the Church could drag me out of hell, but only love and good faith, and my own just judgements.')[13]

Here it is, the love, the truthfulness and the justice of the man which frees him from hell, rather than the prayers of the pope; or as the passage expresses it later, 'leel love and lyvying in truthe'. And this love has an all-inclusive, an ontological value. It is based on our Lord's command to love our neighbour as ourself, a command which itself reflects and reveals the common nature which we share with one another and with him. Here is one of the major themes of the whole poem.

Whose leneth noght, he loveth noght, Oure Lord woot the sothe
And comaundeth ech creature to conformen hym to lovye
His neighebour as hymselve and his enemyes after . . .

45

For oure joy and oure [ju]ele, Jesu Crist of hevene,
In a povere mannes apparaille pursueth us evere,
And loketh on us in hir liknesse and that with lovely chere,
To knowen us by oure kynde herte and castynge of oure
    eighen,
Wheither we love the lordes here bifore the Lord of blisse . . .
For alle are we Cristes creatures, and of his cofres riche,
And bretheren as of oo blood, aswel beggeres as erles.
For at Calvarie of Cristes blood Cristendom gan sprynge. . . .

(If any man does not give, he does not love. And God
commands us to conform our souls to love, and especially to
loving the poor, and after that to loving our enemies . . . For
our joy and our healing, Christ Jesus of Heaven, always
pursues us in a poor man's apparel, and looks upon us in a
poor man's likeness, searching us as we pass with looks of
love, and forever seeking to know us by our kindness of heart;
and he sees which way we cast our eyes, and whether we love
the lords of this earth before the Lord of Heaven. . . . We are
all Christ's creatures, brothers of one blood, beggars as well as
nobles – every one of us wealthy by His coffers. For on
Calvary the whole of Christendom sprang from Christ's
Blood.)[14]

All men are Christ's blood brethren, not only those who are
baptized, and all men are made rich through him who though he
was rich with all the riches of eternity, yet for our sakes became
poor, accepting all the poverty of our human condition in time.
There is no sentimentality in Langland's vision of Christ in the
poor, he was far too close to poverty himself to be sentimental
about it. Rather there is a profound theological insight; heaven
accepts the poverty of earth, love is so abundant in heaven that it
overflows into this world, and transforms all that is apparently
most base and valueless in it. There is here, we may remark, a
parallel to be drawn with the nineteenth century Russian thought
of Christ as a poor man wandering through Russia. It is a parallel
which could be explored further.

But this discussion of the subject in Passus XI is only a prelude
to its full treatment in Passus XVIII, without question one of the
finest passages in the whole poem. Here the subject is not the

46

salvation of one, but the salvation of many. The poet takes the theme of the harrowing of hell and with unequalled power restates the Church's faith in the mystery of Christ's triumph over death, through death. He tells us of the reality of the incarnation, how

This Jesus of his gentries wol juste in Piers armes
In his helm and in his haubergeon – *humana natura*.

(Jesus, out of chivalry, will joust in Pier's coat-of-arms, and wear his helmet and mail, Human Nature.)[15]

His passion is described with admirable economy

'*Consummatum est*', quod Crist, and comsede for to swoune.
Pitousliche and pale as a prison that deieth;
The Lord of life and of light tho leide hise eighen togideres.
The day for drede withdrough and derk bicam the sonne.
The wal waggede and cleef, and all the world quaved.

(Christ said, 'It is finished' and began to grow fearfully pale, like a prisoner on the point of death. And so the Lord of Life and of Light closed his eyes. Then at once the daylight fled in fear and the sun became dark; the wall of the Temple shook and split, and the whole earth quaked.)[16]

But Langland goes further.
We are taken to a strange underworld, to await the final outcome of the combat between death and life. In Psalm 85 there are two verses which run: 'Mercy and truth are met together; righteousness and peace have kissed each other. Truth shall flourish out of the earth; and righteousness hath looked down from heaven.' By long tradition these lines had been taken to refer to the incarnation. The psalm is used at the feast of Christmas. But here Langland applies them to this moment. He shows us two maidens, Mercy coming from the West and Truth from the East, meeting to enquire what is about to happen. Mercy explains that the child that was born of Mary is about to overcome death.

That man shall man save thorugh a maydenes helpe,
And that was tynt thorugh tree, tree shal it wynne,
And that Deeth down broughte, deeth shal releve.
'That thow tellest', quod Truthe, 'is but a tale of waltrot!

47

For Adam and Eve and Abraham with othere
Patriarkes and prophetes that in peyne liggen,
Leve thow nevere that yon light hem aloft brynge,
Ne have hem out of helle – hold thi tonge, Mercy!
It is but trufle that thow tellest – I, Truthe, woot the sothe.
For that is ones in helle, out cometh it never. . . .

    (. . . that mankind should be saved through the help of a
virgin, that a tree should win back what was lost by a tree, and
a death should raise up those whom death had cast down

    'What a lot of clap-trap!' said Truth. 'How could that light
raise up Adam and Eve, Abraham and all the patriarchs and
prophets who lie in pain? What power has it to draw them out
of hell? Hold your tongue, Mercy, and stop talking nonsense!
I am Truth and I know the truth. Once in hell, no man ever
comes out again. . . .')[17]

Mercy replies to this force of conviction with an argument from
experience; poisons can be used to cure poisons, so it may be in
this case.

So shal grace that all bigan make a good ende.

    (. . . so Grace, which was with man at the beginning, will
beguile the Devil in turn. . . .)[18]

Let us wait, says Truth, since here from the North comes
Righteousness; and here from the South replies Mercy, comes Peace
'clothed in patience'.

Rightwisnesse hire reverenced for hir riche clothyng
And preide Pees to telle hire to what place she wolde
And in hire gaye garnements whom she grete thoughte?
'My wil is to wende', quod she, 'and welcome hem alle
That many day myghte I noght se for merknesse of synne
Adam and Eve and othere mo in helle,
Moyses and many mo; Mercy shul [synge),
And I shall daunce therto – do thow so, suster!
For Jesus jestede wel, joye bigynneth dawe:
Ad vesperum demorabitur fletus, et ad matutinum leticia.
Love, that is my lemman, swiche lettres me sente
That Mercy, my suster, and I mankynde sholde save,

And that God hath forgyve and graunted me, Pees, and Mercy
To be mannes meynpernour for everemoore after.
Lo, here the patente! quod Pees, *'pace in idipsum,'*
And that this dede shall dure, *dormiam et requiescam.'*
'What ravestow?' quod Rightwisnesse; 'or thow art right
dronke!
Levestow that yond light unlouke myghte helle
And save mannes soules? Suster, wene it nevere!

(. . . Righteousness looked at her rich attire and greeted her
politely, asking her where she was off to in these gay clothes.
  'I am on my way to welcome all the lost souls', she said,
'whom I have not seen for many a long day now, because of
the darkness of sin. For Adam and Eve and Moses and many
more of those in hell are to have a pardon. And oh, how I
shall be dancing with joy when I see them – and you, dear
sister, must come and dance too. Jesus has fought well, and
joy is dawning at last: "Weeping may endure for a night, but
joy cometh in the morning." For Charity, my lover, has sent
me a letter to say that my sister Mercy and I are to save
mankind – God has given us permission to stand bail for them
forever. See, here is the warrant, and these are the actual
words, "I will both lay me down in peace," and, to make sure
the deed is lasting, "and rest secure".'
  'Have you gone off your head?' said Righteousness, 'or had
too much to drink! Do you really suppose that this light can
unlock hell, and save the souls of men? Don't you believe
it! . . .)[19]

And Righteousness goes on to expound the irrevocable nature of
God's judgement on man's sin.

'And I shall preie', quod Pees, 'Hir peyne moot have ende,
And wo into wele mowe wenden at the laste. . . .'

('But', said Peace, 'I can prove that their pain must come to
an end, and suffering is bound to turn to happiness in the
end.')[20]

We never know what joy is without sorrow, nor light without

darkness, she argues, so it is that with these people their folly and sin will teach them the true nature and value of bliss.

There follows an anxious exchange between the powers of hell, Satan and Lucifer, as to what the light which they see appraoching can mean.

Eft the light bad unlouke, and Lucifer answerede,
'*Quis est iste?*
What lord artow?' quod Lucifer. The light soone seide,
'*Rex glorie,*
The lord of myght and of mayn and alle manere vertues –
Dominus virtutum.
Dukes of this dymme place, anoon undo thise yates,
That Crist may come in, the Kynges sone of Hevene!'
And with that breeth helle brak, with Belialles barres –
For any wye or warde, wide open the yates.
Patriarkes and prophetes, *populus in tenebris,*
Songen Seint Johanes song, '*Ecce Agnus Dei!*'
Lucifer loke ne myghte, so light hym ablente.
And tho that Oure Lord lovede, into his light he laughte, . . .

('Then again the light bade them unlock the gates, and Lucifer answered, saying, "What lord art thou? – Who is this King. . . .?"

' "The King of Glory", answered the Light at once; "the Lord of power and might, and king of every virtue. Unbar the gates quickly, you lords of this dreary place, so that Christ, the Son of the King of Heaven, may enter."

'With that word, Hell itself, and all the bars of Belial, burst asunder, and the gates flew open in the face of the guards. And all the patriarchs and prophets, "the people that sat in darkness", sang aloud the hymn of St John the Baptist: *Ecce agnus dei* – Behold the Lamb of God". But Lucifer could not look to see, for the Light had blinded his eyes. And then our Lord caught up into his light all those that loved him.'[21]

The Lord then claims that he has rightly beguiled Lucifer who himself in the beginning had beguiled mankind.

Now bigynneth thi gile ageyn thee to turne
And my grace to growe ay gretter and widder.

50

The bitternesse that thow hast browe, now brouke it thiselve;
That art doctour of deeth, drynk that thow madest!
  'For I that am lord of life, love is my drynke,
And for that drynke today, I deide upon erthe.
I faught so, me thursteth yet, for mannes soule sake;
May no drynke me moiste, ne my thurst slake,
Till the vendage falle in the vale of Josaphat,
That I drynke right ripe must, *resureccio mortuorum*.
And thanne shal I come as a kyng, crowned, with aungeles,
And have out of helle alle mennes soules . . .
Ac to be merciable to man thanne, my kynde it asketh,
For we beth bretheren of blood, but noght in baptisme
alle . . .
And my mercy shal be shewed to many of my bretheren;
For blood may suffre blood both hungry and acale,
Ac blood may noght se blood blede, but hym rewe,'
    Audivi archana verba que non licet homini loqui.
  'Ac my rightwisnesse and right shal rule al helle,
And mercy al mankynde bifore me in hevene.
For I were an unkynde kyng but I my kyn helpe – . . .

(' "At last your guile begins to turn against you, while my
grace grows ever wider and greater. The bitterness that you
have brewed, you shall drink yourself; you that are doctor of
death, shall swallow your own medicine!

    "For I, the Lord of Life, drink no drink but love, and for
that drink I died today on earth. I have fought so hard for
man's soul that I am still thirsty, and no drink can ever refresh
me or quench my thirst, till the vintage fall in the valley of
Jehoshaphat, so that I may drink the ripe new wine of the
resurrection of the dead. Then I shall come as a king, crowned
with angels, and draw all mens's souls out of hell. . . .

    "And how can I, with my human nature, refuse men mercy
on that day? For we are brothers of one blood, though we are
not all of one baptism. . . .

    ". . . And then my mercy will be shown to many of my
brethren. For a man may suffer his kind to go cold and
hungry, but he cannot see them bleed without pitying them."

('And I heard secret words which it is not granted to man to utter.)

' "My righteousness and my justice shall rule over hell, and my mercy over all mankind before me in Heaven. I should be an inhuman king if I refused help to my own brethren. . . ." ')[22]

There is much that could be said about this passage from the point of view of its style. We might consider the masterly contrast between the 'doctor of death' and 'Lord of life', or the brilliant use of Latin phrases, mostly from the Liturgy of Holy Week, which adds a particular solemnity to it. But its contents are still more striking.

The line *Audivi verba archana*, . . . may be taken to imply Langland's boldest claim to divine inspiration, since he here takes to himself the words of St Paul, as A. V. C. Schmidt suggests. The introduction of this line at this moment of climax certainly suggests that it had great importance for the poet. But it may also mean that Langland had received some inner assurance about the salvation of all, which he refrains from making explicit. All that Christ says explicitly is that he may have mercy on all, and that those who have sinned will suffer in Purgatory before they are released. But the thirst of Christ for the salvation of all, and the solidarity of humankind in him, so powerfully expressed, have many implications.

The lines:

For blood may suffre blood both hungry and acale,
Ac blood may noght se blood blede, but hym rewe,

may forcibly recall to us an incident in the life of the Staretz Sylvan. When in the Russian monastery on Athos during the 1920's the conversation turned to the fate of unbelievers after death – and surely the militant godless of the Soviet Union were in mind – one monk declared with evident satisfaction. 'God will punish all atheists. They will burn in everlasting fire'. 'Love could not bear that', was the Staretz' reply, 'We must pray for all.' But when asked to expand he refused to say more.[23]

That the dramatic form of Langland's passus, very marked in the original, owes something to the mystery plays of his period is almost certain. In many things he is very much a man of his own time and place. But the theology of the poem at this crucial point reminds us in many ways of the theology of the Eastern Church, of which he can have had only the most indirect knowledge. In Eastern Orthodoxy the prayer and hope that all may be saved has a stronger place in the tradition than in the West. The faith that Christ's solidarity with all men in life and death involves the raising up of all men through the harrowing of hell is much more strongly expressed in the Church's worship and teaching. The harrowing of hell, and the raising of Adam are all one action. We can see this in the third of the prayers said at Vespers on the feast of Pentecost. We can see it also in the rites of Holy Week which we shall examine in a later chapter. Here for example are three verses from the Mattins of Holy Saturday in the Byzantine rite to illustrate this faith:

> To earth hast thou come down, O Master, to save Adam, and not finding him on earth, thou hast descended into hell, seeking him there.
> Uplifted on the Cross, thou has uplifted with thyself all living men; and then descending beneath the earth thou raisest up all that lie buried there.
> The whole creation was altered by thy Passion; for all things suffered with thee, knowing, O Lord, that thou holdest all in unity.[24]

At the other end of Christendom, in the same century as *Piers Plowman*, the iconographic art of the Eastern Church reached new heights of expressiveness. In the great figure of the risen Christ drawing up Adam and Eve from death in the apse of the Church of St Saviour in Chora (Karieh Djami) in the city of Constantinople, we have the perfect visual equivalent to the words of William Langland. As we have already seen in the case of Julian of Norwich, when this writing is seen in the context of the Eastern Christian tradition, it no longer looks marginal or fanciful. Rather it is seen to belong at the very heart of orthodox Christianity.

In this chapter we have thought of the fourteenth century in England, and have hinted at the way in which that century has been alive in our own time, not only in the work of T. S. Eliot. Its influence in the work of David Jones is even more clearly to be seen. Much of what has been said of the first poetic flowering of this period in England, could also have been said of the similar achievement in Scotland about one century later. In the poets of that late fifteenth century period, Henryson, Dunbar, and Douglas there is a similar fulness. In Henryson we have a vision of the unity of man with all creation in the providence of God. In Dunbar we find one of the last and most powerful of all medieval affirmations of Christ's conquest over death. These writers have also had a strong influence in our own time. But I believe that the real value of this latter period for all who inherit the tradition of the languages of England and Scotland, is yet to be realized. Just as in Constantinople, in the last years of the Eastern Empire, the genius of writers and painters, of mystics and theologians flamed up into new and unexpected works of creation, so in Scotland as the old order came to an end, there was a last brilliant portrayal of the medieval synthesis. One of its final expressions, is to be found in the great heraldic ceiling in St Machar's Cathedral in Aberdeen. There in 1520, the Bishop, Gavin Dunbar, erected a flat ceiling of panelled oak with forty eight shields, arranged in carefully thought-out order. We see in it the Scottish Church in communion with the apostolic see of Rome, the Kingdom of Scotland in its rightful place, within the order of Western Christendom, the Scottish nobility giving structure to the society of a sovereign people.[25] It represents a noble if fragile vision of unity and order affirmed in the very years when, at least at the religious level, that order was breaking up. It is a vision of unity and order which as we shall see in the next chapter was still alive in Aberdeen a century later, despite all the turmoil of the intervening years.

Chapter 3

'The Six-days' World Transposing in an Hour'

We turn now from the fourteenth century to the first half of the seventeenth, a period which is no less important from the national, religious and literary point of view, but is a period of much greater complexity. We begin with a poem which itself suggests something of the quality of thought and reflection which this time contains:

Prayer, the Church's banquet, angels' age,
God's breath in man returning to his birth,
The soul in paraphrase, heart in pilgrimage,
The Christian plummet sounding heav'n and earth;
Engine against the Almighty, sinners' tower,
Reversed thunder, Christ-side-piercing spear,
The six-days' world transposing in an hour,
A kind of tune, which all things hear and fear;
Softness and peace, and joy, and love, and bliss,
Exalted manna, gladness of the best,
Heaven in ordinary, man well drest,
The milkie way, the bird of paradise,
Church bells beyond the stars heard, the soul's blood,
The land of spices; something understood.[1]

The poem 'Prayer', is one of extraordinary richness both of thought and imagery. Among many other things its exemplifies what Eliot says about the relation of tradition to the individual talent of the writer. Some of George Herbert's images are startlingly

55

new and original, 'Church bells beyond the stars heard', 'the milky way'; others are more traditional and familiar, 'God's breath in man', 'sinners' tower'. By their juxtaposition they suggest the work of a man who has made the tradition his own in a highly personal way, one for whom praying and thinking are indissolubly connected. He is one who cares about orthodoxy, not as a static repetition of past expressions but as a living, growing pattern of truth. They suggest that fusion of thought and feeling which is so strong a feature of the writing of this century and which is one of the things which drew Eliot to it.

There are many ways in which we might regard this period from the point of view of the Anglican tradition. It was marked in its later years by Archbishop Laud's unsuccessful and in many ways unskilful attempts to impose a certain uniformity on English worship. It was marked as a time of massive scholarly activity. Following on the classical work of Richard Hooker (1554–1600) which only began to be assimilated in the years following his death, it saw the beginnings of a distinctively Anglican theological position, on the one side clearly distinguished from that of counter-reformation Rome, on the other from that of Calvinist Geneva. Above all it was marked by a renewal of the understanding and the practice of the Christian way of common and private prayer. And all these things were held together in a single focus.

In many ways the period may be summed up in the person and work of one man, Lancelot Andrewes, Bishop of Winchester (1555–1626). It is not by chance that Eliot entitled the small book of essays published in 1928, in which he announced his return to the Christian faith, *For Lancelot Andrewes*. The central place of Andrewes in the development of Eliot's own religious position is a theme which has not yet been adequately studied. It was certainly a major factor in leading him to ask for baptism in the Church of England. For Eliot, Andrewes embodied in himself the learning, the theology and the devotion which marks the best men of this age.

The achievement of Hooker and Andrewes was to make the English Church more worthy of intellectual assent. No religion can survive the judgment of history unless the best minds of its time have collaborated in its construction; if the Church of Elizabeth is worthy of the age of Shakespeare and Jonson, this is because of the work of Hooker and Andrewes. . . . In both Hooker and Andrewes – the latter was the friend and intimate of Casaubon – we find also that breadth of culture, an ease with humanism and Renaissance learning, which helped to put them on terms of equality with their continental antagonists and to elevate their Church above the position of a local heretical sect.[2]

Here was the sense of a classical, universal order which for Eliot was so vital. In the sermons and prayers of Lancelot Andrewes, as in the theology of Hooker, as in the actual life and worship of the period, Eliot found signs of a Catholicism which was not ignorant either of the Renaissance or the Reformation, a tradition which, in that sense, had already moved into the modern world, and lived on our side of the gulf which separates us from the Middle Ages. It was a way of living and thinking the Christian tradition which had taken humanism and criticism into itself, without being destroyed by them. 'A Catholicism *without* the element of humanism and criticism' as Eliot remarks elsewhere in this book, 'would be a Catholicism of despair.'[3] Such a Catholicism, which in the period following the modernist crisis of the early part of this century was much in evidence in the Roman Catholic Church, a Catholicism powerful and assertive, but narrow and authoritarian, could not win his assent, however much he might admire elements within it. The Catholic whole, he was convinced, must be something larger and more inclusive than that. One can only speculate as to the way in which he would have reacted to our present situation in which a more open and self-critical form of Catholicism is much more evidently at work within the Roman Church than it was in the period between the two Vatican Councils. Certainly, one may suppose, he would have seen signs here of a deeper and less arrogant hope.

In Andrewes and in the Church from which he came, he thought to hear, 'the voice of a man . . . who speaks with the old authority and the new culture'. In the theology of his school we find, 'a determination to stick to essentials, that awareness of the needs of the times, the desire for clarity and precision in matters of importance, and the indifference to matters indifferent' which seemed to him to indicate the true balance and openness of tradition and to be no less necessary in the twentieth than in the seventeenth century. Above all he found in the theology of this period a willingness to question, to recognize the uncertainties which surround even our deepest certainties, and this was another of the things which most of all drew him to the poetry and preaching of these men.

Not that the willingness to leave many questions open and unsettled implies any denial of the reality of man's knowledge of God. The apparent openness of seventeenth century Anglicanism does not proceed from a lack of commitment in the fundamental areas of Christian faith. To recognize our own uncertainties can be a mark of realism and humility, and can make us in the end more willing to acknowledge the great but mysterious certainties of God. Through all the vicissitudes of his relationship with God, Herbert can conclude at the end of the poem we have quoted 'Something understood'. And Eliot in his essay on Andrewes does not hesitate to use the word 'contemplative' of him, discerning in him the qualities of a true mystic, a word which Eliot avoids, presumably on account of the innumerable ways in which it has been misused. Andrewes, he affirms, was one who *saw* into the mysteries which he was expounding, one indeed who lived within them. 'When Andrewes begins his sermon, from beginning to end you are sure that he is wholly in his subject, unaware of anything else, that the emotion grows as he penetrates more deeply into his subject, that he is finally "alone with the Alone", with the mystery which he is seeking to grasp more and more firmly. . . . Andrewes' emotion is purely contemplative; it is not personal, it is wholly evoked by the object of contemplation to which it is adequate; his emotion is wholly contained in and explained by its object.' [4] Allowing for the fact that behind the words which Eliot chooses here, there lie certain fiercely debated literary issues, we may surely also see in this passage a remarkable description of that 'dogmatic-ecstatic' quality, that quality of being carried out beyond oneself into that which is contemplated, which is characteristic of the whole Christian mystical tradition.

And being carried out of himself into God, Andrewes' own thought, prayer and life, begin to acquire, within all the limitations and fragility of the human condition, some element of the divine. God is one yet manifold, his grace brings unity and reconciliation without destroying diversity and multiplicity. Something of that quality appears in Andrewes' preaching. J. B. Mosley in an essay written at the height of the Oxford Movement and published in *The British Critic* in January 1842, comments:

> He is so quick and varied, so dexterous and rich in his combinations; he brings facts, types, prophecies and doctrines together with such rapidity; groups, arranges, systematizes, sets and resets them with such readiness of movement, that he seems to have a kind of ubiquity, and to be everywhere and in every part of the system at the same time. . . . He has everything in his head at once; not in the sense in which a puzzle-headed person may be said to have, who has *every idea* confused in his mind because he has *no one idea clear*, but like a man who is at once clear-headed and *manifold* . . . in his ideas, who can do more than apprehend one point clearly or many dimly – can apprehend, that is to say, many keenly. [5]

Here we have a description of something we may call a qualitative Catholicity of understanding. This is a view of things which is complete not through the mere inclusion of all the necessary articles of faith, but through a perception of their coherence with one another, or rather of their co-inherence in one another, so that, for instance, we may see all implicitly present in the original confession that Jesus is Lord. So in his exposition of the Christian faith Andrewes draws the many into one. The testimonies of scripture and tradition, the interplay of the different articles of faith, the consideration of the different patterns of language, in Hebrew, Greek, Latin, English, are united in a coherent structure. It is just the same with his *Preces Privatae*. We are conscious at once of the many-sided quality of prayer, its different aspects and elements, praise, thanksgiving, commemoration, confession, intercession, adoration. Everything here begins from God and ends in him, and all is seen in a universal perspective. Not that this width of view involves a neglect of the particular gifts and callings of God. Here in the intercessions there is a gathering together of men and women of all kinds, of every human circumstance, a detailed enumeration of all those for whom Andrewes felt bound to pray and give thanks. And in the very structure of the prayers, with their liberal use of the Byzantine liturgical texts as well as of material provided by the

Bible and by the Latin tradition, there is evident the same concern to gather together the many into one. As R. W. Church remarks:

> He felt himself, even in private prayer, one of the great body of God's creation and God's Church. He reminded himself of it, as he did of the object of his worship, in the profession of his faith. He acted on it in his detailed and minute intercessions. . . . The poetical and imaginative side of his nature shows itself in the vivid pictures which he calls up, . . . of the glories of nature, and the wonder of God's kingdom, its history, its manifold organization.[6]

It is important to stress that this is a drawing together of the whole world of nature, with the world of human history and existence. In both realms God's activity is to be seen. For gathered together in Christ there are not only the centuries which preceded his coming, the centuries recorded in the Old Testament, and the centuries which flow from it, the centuries of the Church's life, but also the fulness of the natural order, the round of the seasons, as well as the events of history. And all this is made accessible to us in the Church's prayer, for in prayer man acts as priest of creation, bringing before God the praise of all that is made. Above all this is true of the heart of Christian prayer, in the sacrament of the Eucharist where temporal and eternal are joined together into one.

Let me quote from Andrewes himself at the end of a sermon preached at Christmas, where as so often he applies the whole theme of his sermon to the sacrament which is about to be celebrated:

> There [at the altar] we do not gather to Christ or of Christ, but we gather Christ himself; and, gathering him we shall gather the tree and fruit and all upon it. For, as there is a recapitulation of all in heaven and earth in Christ, so there is a recapitulation of all in Christ in the Holy Sacrament. You may see it clearly. There is in Christ the Word eternal, for things in heaven; there is also flesh, for things on earth. Semblably, the sacrament consisteth of a heavenly and of a terrene part (it is Irenaeus' own words); the heavenly – there the Word too, the abstract of the other; the earthly – the element. And in the elements, you may observe there is a fulness of the seasons of the natural year; of

60

the corn-flour or harvest in the one, bread; of the wine-press or vintage in the other, wine. And in the heavenly, of the wheat-corn whereto he compareth himself – bread, even the Living Bread that came down from heaven; the true Manna, whereof we may gather each his gomer. And again, of him, the true Vine as he calls himself – the blood of the grapes of that vine. And both these issuing out of this day's recapitulation, both in *corpus autem aptasti mihi* of this day.[7]

Behind this passage there lies very evidently the reformation controversy about transubstantiation. Andrewes in no way wishes to diminish belief in the real presence of Christ in the sacrament. On that point he is at one with his Roman Catholic adversaries. But he believes that there is a way of understanding the Eucharist which will do justice to the reality of the gifts offered by man, the bread and the wine, product of human labour as well as of the round of the seasons, and that this is more fully in accord with the proportion of faith than a way of understanding which to him at least seems to deny or undervalue the earthly aspect of the sacrament. But what is more striking here is the affirmation of the gathering together in Christ of the times of the natural order, seed-time and harvest, as well as of the times of the history of God's kingdom. This is indeed an enlargement of what is meant by *anamnesis*, the recalling of all that God has done both in creation and redemption. Here are insights which speak directly to our twentieth century concern with ecology, and which show us yet again, the inclusive, unifying power of Christian prayer.

In our own day Thomas Merton has written, 'If I can unite *in myself* the thought and the devotion of Eastern and Western Christendom, the Greek and the Latin fathers, the Russian with the Spanish mystics, I can prepare in myself the reunion of divided Christians. From that secret and unspoken unity in myself can eventually come a visible and manifest unity of all Christians'.[8] Andrewes in his life and prayer was doing just this. In a situation of division and polemic, a situation to which he himself at times contributed, the deepest movement of his life was in a different direction. As he prayed for the whole Christian family, 'for the Catholic Church, its establishment and increase; for the Eastern, its deliverance and union; for the Western, its adjustment and peace; for the British, the supply of what is wanting in it, the strengthening of that which remains in it',[9] he was advancing that secret and unspoken unity in himself, he was making real the calling of the bishop to be a representative man, a man who draws together and unites in himself the many callings and ages of mankind. More, he was becoming aware of himself as 'one of the great body of God's creation'. He brings with him before God, the praise of all creation, and so fulfils the basic calling of man.

If Lancelot Andrewes in some ways is the representative figure of the Anglicanism of this time, then Little Gidding is certainly the representative place. It was not for nothing that Eliot called the last of his *Quartets Little Gidding*, for the life of the Ferrar family there in the years before the Civil War sums up many of the most notable qualities of the Anglicanism of that time. It was to a remarkable degree a conjunction of apparent opposites. It was an extended family of three generations, which for a number of years led a life of an intensity of prayer and devotion which would outstrip many monasteries. It was a centre of study as well as devotion and yet it was also a centre of practical and pastoral concern for its neighbours. It was at once of its own time, and yet full of a timeless peace and serenity. It was above all a place which in no way advertised itself and yet became known, which attracted many people, and especially the young. Poets and scholars came there, notable among them Richard Crashaw. George Herbert was most intimately connected with the family. It was to Nicholas Ferrar that he entrusted the manuscript of his poems, leaving it in his hands as to whether or not to publish them. There was an indefinable beauty about the place and its life which many different people felt. As a friendly observer exclaimed, 'God be glorified for such, whose prayers were powerful and incessant to pierce the heavens. The whole land was better for their sanctity. They fasted, that famine might not be inflicted upon our common gluttony. . . . They kept vigil all night, that the day of the Lord might not come upon us unawares, that sleep in security. The whole world was better for their contempt of the world.'[10]

Here indeed was a 'mid winter spring', a moment without apparent antecedents or immediate successors, a moment, before the devastations of the civil war, when much was given and received. 'The six-days' world', the world of God's creation in which man is called to work together with God, the world of man's daily, recurrent labour, was 'transposed', transformed by the sense of the redeeming, recreating power of God, made known within it through man's response of prayer and praise. The gifts of many ages were gathered up in one, into the day of the Lord's triumph over death and over all that tends to bind down and destroy the life of man. In his poem called 'Easter', Herbert asks:

Can there be any day but this
Though many suns to shine endeavour?
We count three hundred but we miss
There is but one, and that one ever. . . .[11]

II

What is too little realized is that contemporary with this effort of rediscovery and reconstitution taking place in England, a similar effort was being made in Scotland and in particular in Aberdeen under the aegis of one of the greatest bishops of the Scottish tradition, Patrick Forbes, Bishop of Aberdeen from 1618–1635. Here within a brief twenty years and within the narrow compass of a single city, geographically remote and numerically insignificant, there was a movement of intellectual and spiritual activity which for a time made Aberdeen one of the theological centres of Europe. In the persons of John Forbes of Corse, the son of Bishop Patrick, and of William Forbes, professor in Aberdeen, then briefly first Bishop of Edinburgh, it produced two theologians of unquestionably international importance. Here again was a moment when something of universal significance was revealed within the limitations of a particular time and place.

One of the many interesting facts about this episode, is that though it provides fascinating parallels with what was going on in England, it seems to have developed very much in independence from it. The cultural and commercial links of Scotland at that time were with continental Europe rather than with England. Both John and William Forbes spent long years of study in the Low Countries, in Germany and in the world of French-speaking Protestantism;

they show a detailed knowledge of the theological debate as it was carried on on the continent. Whether from policy or from actual isolation they show less concern with what was going on in England.

Nonetheless comparisons between the two developments almost impose themselves. We find in Scotland as in England the same combination of deep devotion, practical pastoral concern and care for historical and theological scholarship. In Aberdeen there was, if anything, an even more determined and conscious effort to find ways of reconciliation, first within the already divided world of the Reformation, then even across the gulf between the Reformation and Rome. The first of John Forbes' major works, *The Irenicum*, is an attempt not only to defend the liturgical provisions of the Perth Articles of 1618, but as its name suggests, an effort to set out a way of reconciliation between the episcopal and presbyterian forms of government. The task is performed with immense skill and immense learning. As the son of a distinguished Bishop, and at the same time a man who had received ordination at the hands of a Presbytery in Holland, John Forbes could appreciate the strength of both systems. But he is clear that the presbyteral college needs a permanent president or moderator, and that a church which lacks such figures, while it does not cease to be a church, labours under what he terms an administrative or 'economic' defect.

One of the striking things about Forbes' arguing of this case is the space which he gives not only to the views of the early fathers but also to the positions of the medieval Latin writers. As E. G. Selwyn remarks:

> No Anglican writer leaves one with a stronger sense of the continuity of Christian life and tradition in the Reformed Church than this scholar of Aberdeen, or brings out more clearly . . . . the large area of common ground which Catholic and Protestant shared. . . . Forbes' mind is in close contact, not only with Scripture and antiquity – and it is said that he never inserted a reference in his text without verifying it – but also with the great minds of the Middle Ages: with Peter Lombard, Gratian, Aquinas, Bonaventure, Scotus, Durandus. We feel in his pages what the development of Christian thought in the West might have been, if events had not forestalled it and split its progress.[12]

In Scotland no less than in England, the appeal to the fathers and the schoolmen as secondary but vital authorities, was used as a way of escape from an arbitrary biblicism, and as a means of discerning in contemporary controversy between essentials and inessentials. It was not enough to know the thought of one period alone. The whole effort of historical study, massively set out in Forbes' *Instructiones Historico-Theologicae*, was intended to provide criteria for judging between constantly dissentient and increasingly intolerant schools of thought. To quote Selwyn again, 'He takes his stand on no private judgement of the meaning of Scripture, but makes his constant appeal to the Fathers of the undivided Church. The abundant patristic *testimonia* which he cites are for him *indices* of the mind of the whole Church throughout many centuries, and it is that mind which he desires to express and transmit'.[13]

If John Forbes may lay claim to be the greatest scholar amongst the men of Aberdeen, I believe that it is William Forbes whom we must judge to have been the most far-seeing of them. For one thing his vision reaches not only to a reconciliation between the different schools within the Protestant world, but to the restoration of unity with Rome itself. For another thing, his great work the *Considerationes Modestae* shows an unusual awareness of the harm which polemic and controversy was doing to the very texture of theology itself. From his theological writings, from the noble and poignant plea for the restoration of the peace of Christendom to be found in the memorable sermon which he preached before Charles I in Edinburgh in 1633, we get the impression of a man of exceptional sensitivity and perception. It is an impression which is confirmed by Gilbert Burnet's tribute to his character, a tribute all the more striking because coupled with a distinct disclaimer of Forbes' eirenic attitudes towards Rome. 'My father, that knew him long, and being his council for him in his law-matters, had occasion to know him well, has often told me, that he never saw him but he thought his heart was in heaven, and he was never alone with him but he felt within himself a commentary on those words of the apostles, "Did not our hearts burn within us, while he yet talked with us, and opened the Scriptures?" '[14] In our present climate of opinion, where everywhere the broken dialogue between Rome and the Reformation is being taken up again, the importance of William

Forbes' pioneering work may perhaps come to be recognized more widely.

But rather than dwell on the writings of either John or William Forbes, I intend to turn to the work of one of the lesser known writers of their school, James Sibbald. So far as I know his work has never caught the attention of historians or theologians, a fact which is strange in view of the quality which it reveals. I intend to concentrate our attention primarily on the sermon which he preached in 1635 in tribute to the memory of Bishop Patrick Forbes, the man whose judgement and determination, vision and good sense had made the whole eirenic and constructive effort of these years possible. At first sight the sermon might appear an example of an excessive display of baroque eloquence and erudition. To understand it we need to place it within its own context, see it in relation to Sibbald's other sermons preached in Aberdeen in the same period.

Above all we need to see this statement about the Church's ministry in relation to the whole attempt to recapitulate the tradition in the present, to make clear its underlying unity despite the divisions which have occurred. Only thus shall we see the true seriousness and the true beauty of Sibbald's work. In his celebration of the life and achievement of the bishop, he proclaims, as we shall see, both his belief in the unity of the tradition and also his belief in the transcendent greatness and glory of man's life when it is lived in union with God's purpose in creation and redemption. Since the texts which we shall be citing are not at all easily accessible, I shall quote them at some length. In this way we can get something of the flavour and quality of the original, and also allow a voice which has been silent for three hundred years to be heard again.

James Sibbald was born towards the end of the sixteenth century, and took full part in the spiritual and intellectual movement which marked Aberdeen in the 1620s and '30s. He seems to have been particularly closely linked with William Forbes. It was one of the charges made against him at the time of his ejection from his office in 1639. All that we have from his hand, apart from the funeral sermon for the Bishop, and a set of theses used for his doctoral disputation in 1627, are the sermons published in 1658 almost a decade after Sibbald's death in exile in Dublin. These sermons were published at the request of those who had heard them preached, and the very fact of their publication is a tribute to the esteem in which Sibbald was held by his fellow townsmen, twenty years after he had been silenced. The volume is dedicated to the Provost, Baillies and other Councillors of the city, in order that it might enjoy their protection. For though the matter and the manner of the sermons is not, in general, controversial, some of their particular emphases can hardly have been fashionable in the latter years of the Commonwealth. Sibbald has a great longing for unity, unity in the Church and in civil society, and this is a theme which recurs. As we shall suggest his whole approach to theology implies a search for reconciliation.

The style of the parochial sermons in simpler and less polished than that of the funeral oration, but quotations from the Fathers are still quite numerous, above all from Augustine. 'The learned Calvin' is cited only once. In these sermons too, we find a thoroughly sacramental view of Christian life and worship, a view in which man is called to work together with God. For Sibbald, it is Christ himself who is the sacrament of man's meeting with God. All the other sacraments of God's love, and in the wider meaning of the word they are many, have their purpose and their power from him. Through them all, man in his totality is taken up into union with his Creator. And all this sacramental economy is centred in the Eucharist. Speaking of the duty of thanksgiving, revealed already under the law, he declares, 'Under the gospel now, I may say, it is yet more necessary. The proper sacrifice of Christians is the sacrifice of praise and thanksgiving, everywhere vehemently urged in the New Testament. Our blessed Lord did institute the blessed sacrament of his body and blood giving thanks, and for this end that we may give thanks to God, as for all his benefits, so especially for that of redemption. By the right performance of this duty, we begin our heaven on earth, for the proper exercise of heaven is praise'.[15] Praise indeed is one of Sibbald's favourite themes.

While this economy centres on the Eucharist it is by no means confined there. In places, Sibbald prefers the Greek term 'mysteries' to the Latin 'sacraments', possibly on account of its New Testament connotations, possibly too on account of its wider and more flexible range of meaning. We see here in practice how the historical learning of these men enabled them to be freer than many of their contemporaries in the exposition of the gospel. There is a remarkable passage which comes towards the end of a sermon preached at the celebration of the sacrament, where we see how generously he understands this term:

There is an unspeakable sweetness in God in his divine mysteries and obedience, which may be tasted by the soul of a spiritual man. 'O taste and see how sweet the Lord is', saith David, as if he would say, 'If ye taste ye will know the sweetness of his goodness, mercy, liberality and power.' So we may say of every divine mystery, 'Taste and see how sweet it is', and of every virtue, 'Taste and see how sweet is obedience, patience, humility, chastity'. . . . But why do I insist so much upon this? First, to show the admirable goodness of God, who vouchsafeth so many ways to communicate himself to us, and maketh us so many ways able to receive him. All this proceedeth merely from his infinite goodness. . . . Secondly, I have insisted upon this at this time to move you, to stir up all the powers and faculties of your souls, to receive him who offereth himself at this time most abundantly to be participated by us. . . .[16]

There are so many ways in which God comes to meet us, and so many ways in which we may come to meet him in response. In all the mysteries of his love, in all that reveals him to us, we can find the sweetness of his presence. And in all our acts of faith and obedience there is a similar possibility for us to receive him. God draws us to himself, the initiative is always his; and yet our response is real. We can, in a measure, draw him to ourselves, by prayer and repentance, by faith and obedience. 'This draught of us by God is in some sort reciprocal and mutual. As he draweth us, so in some sort we draw him. We draw God to us by our prayers, sighs and groans, yea by them we hold and bind him in a manner. "Let me go", said he to Jacob wrestling with him, "for the day approacheth". "Let me alone", said he to Moses, "that my anger may wax hot". Thus by every virtue, patience, chastity, mercy, etc., and by every good work, we draw God in some measure to us, who the better we are, draweth the nearer to us, and delighteth the more in us. But especially we draw him to us by love, which God himself who is love doth alway accompany. "He that abideth in love abideth in God and God abideth in him", saith St John. "If any man love me", saith our Lord, "I will love him, and my Father will love him, and my Father and I will come and dwell with him." Thus being drawn by God we draw him to us in some measure, but yet absolutely we draw not him, but by him are drawn unto himself. For it is he who giveth us all that strength of beauty, virtue and love which pleaseth him, and he giveth it for this effect, that we may be united more and more to him wherein our happiness standeth.' [17]

In such a passage, with its carefully balanced statement of the way in which on the basis of God's gift there is a real movement of co-operation on the part of man, we can see a practical working out of the detailed analysis of the controversies about the doctrine of justification by faith which we find, for instance, in William Forbes' *Considerationes Modestae*. While there is no opening for a doctrine of human merit, there is a recognition that man can receive gifts from God which begin to transform his nature. In these gifts of God which truly become our own, there is a real participation in the life and nature of God. We can see here a very patristic attitude towards the work of man's salvation, an attitude which we find still more clearly set out in the commemorative sermon for Patrick Forbes, to which we now turn.

The sermon has as its theme, the words 'Holiness to the Lord' which the book of Exodus tells us were inscribed on the gold plate placed on the high priest's crown or mitre, and it begins with a consideration of the significance of crowns. All Christians are to be crowned; for all Christians are made free. Baptism is our liberation from slavery.

> Unspeakable is the matter of joy that we have, through the benefit of baptism; we are free thereby from the servitude of Satan. . . . Yea by it we are advanced not only to liberty but also to the dignity of God's children. . . . If the dignity of all Christians, if their combats, courage and hope be so great, how much more is it with the spiritual rulers, whose duty is to lead and bring them to the crown. . . . Great is their pre-eminence, great and many their battles, wherein if they acquit themselves worthily there abideth for them a far more glorious crown than others (I Peter 5:4). What more divine thing can there be, than to be a

worker with God in procuring the salvation of men, for whom the blood of Christ was shed? 'Of all divine perfections,' saith that old writer that goeth by the name of Dionysius the Areopagite 'it is the most divine to be God's fellow-worker'. . . . How glorious a thing had it been for a man to have been a worker with God in the framing of this world. 'but' (to apply to our purpose the words of Chrysostom) 'God giveth a greater honour to pastors; to whom he saith as it were, I have made heaven and earth, but I give thee power to make earth heaven: I have made clear lights, but make thou more clear: thou canst not make a man, but thou mayest make him gracious and acceptable unto me.' [18]

Already we see outlined the patristic vision of the ministry as a work of co-operation with God, which will be developed in the sermon later. And already we see that what is said of the ordained ministry is set in the context of the ministry of all Christian people. In a way which is remarkably modern Sibbald refuses to see the ordained ministry in isolation from the priesthood of all God's people, and that universal priesthood he sees in terms of the whole creation.

In the latter part of the sermon, Sibbald opens up a remarkably inclusive vision of the work of God as the one who in creation and redemption alike, ceaselessly communicates his own joy to his creatures. It is one of the finest passages in the whole sermon.

Holiness belongeth to God in respect of all that pertain unto him, but especially in respect of men; and amongst these chiefly in respect of the priest and high priest. All this world is, as it were, the temple of his Deity, consecrated to his worship, sanctified by his presence, and filled with his glory (Isaiah 6:3). Everywhere, as it were, we may see him present; and ever, as in his presence, should walk in it as in an holy temple, worshipping, praising and blessing him; for in his temple doth everyone speak of his glory (Psalm 29:9). Even the senseless creatures praise and bless him; because so much as in them lieth, they excite to this duty such as have reason, by their representation of the divine perfections. Herein their goodness and chief use standeth, and for it they were chiefly made. Hence the creatures are called the

70

proclaimers and witnesses of the Deity, whose voice is heard and understood everywhere (Psalm 19: 1–3; Acts 14:17).

The spirits of men are yet more properly his temple; his presence in them is more illustrious than in things bodily; and they may come to him, and be joined to him more excellently than them: there is no soul which is not more capable of him than the whole world besides; therefore the fathers, Nyssen and Chrysostom, mark that God proceeded to the making of man, as it were with deliberation, and drew as it were beforehand his portraiture by his word, showing what a one he should be, and according to what likeness and for what end (Gen. 1:20). He is more especially sanctified unto his divine worship and inhabitation than all things bodily; that converting himself within to his indweller, he may converse with God, worship and adore him. He alone, and the angelical spirits, may know and love him which is true holiness, whereby he dwelleth in them and they become his temple, much more happy and sublime than all this bodily world, which is not sensible of his presence. This knowledge and love unite them unto him by a vital band; thereby 'they are made partakers of his divine nature' (II Peter 1:4). Yea, and thereby are changed in him whom they know and love and become 'one Spirit with him' (I Cor. 6:17). So in them is required a more special holiness.[19]

We observe here how the creation of man, capable of knowing and loving God, is set within the context of the whole act of creation. If Sibbald has a high view of the priesthood of the ordained ministry, it is because he has a high view of the priesthood to which all men and women are called by virtue of their humanity. Here is a cosmic view of God's purposes in the creation of man, a view which does not ignore man's bodily existence nor the physical world in which man finds himself. The tendency to focus on the doctrine of redemption almost to the exclusion of the doctrine of creation is notably absent. We notice too at the end, that the doctrine of *theosis*, of man's becoming god by grace, which is commonly thought to have disappeared in the West, is quietly affirmed, and that the New Testament texts traditionally used to defend it are cited. Here already is a striking instance of how themes from earlier parts of the Christian tradition are re-appearing in Sibbald's teaching.

The same wide perspectives are opened up in his consideration of the doctrine of redemption.

If we consider the restoration of mankind, this will appear more clearly. For in Christ Jesus, God by himself, and not by any created gift sanctifieth the human nature, drawing it above all things created to himself, and substantially uniting it into the person of the Son of God. Therefore the ancients say that by the Deity itself, the manhood of Christ, is *velut igne penetrata et unguento delibuta*, pierced by it, as it were, with fire, and anointed by it, as with ointment; so the divine nature in this union is, as it were, the ointment, and the human nature that which is anointed. Whence also is the name of Christ: 'Christ' saith Nazianzen, 'became man, that he by himself might sanctify men, and might be, as it were, leaven to the whole lump; and that uniting them to himself, who was condemned, he might deliver them from damnation; being made for us all that we are, except sin. The son of man, in respect of whom he came. . . .' 'Christ', saith Augustine. '*Si sacramenta cogites, est sanctus sanctorum; si gregem subditum cogites, est pastor pastorum; si fabricam cogites, est fundamentum fundamentorum*' – the holiest of holies, the pastor of pastors, and the foundation of foundations. This is an admirable and incomprehensible holiness. Here kytheth [is made known] an infinite goodness of God which hath appointed such a fountain of purity and sanctity of mankind. 'Of his fulness we all receive' (John 1:16). By this one all that are made holy are sanctified, as by one all were defiled. From him cometh all holiness to the outward symbols and sacraments, which he hath instituted for us that are rude and led by sense, that by these sensible things he might sanctify us, and by bodily touching he might infuse his Spirit and his gifts in our souls, and faculties thereof; that thence it may break out in all our actions, and so the whole man, and all his life, may be wholly devoted, and consecrated to God; and thereby reduced to him, who is the supreme good and last end, from whom he came and in whom for ever he should rest.[20]

It is a very balanced restatement of the classical teaching of the early centuries about the reconciliation and union of God and man in Christ, a restatement which makes clear the central place of Christ in the whole economy of the Church's life and worship. The highly controversial question, at that time, of the number of the sacraments is put into a proper perspective in a vision of things which sees Christ himself as the origin and centre of the whole sacramental system, a system which spreads out and has its influence through the whole of human life, which at every point involves the body no less than the soul. And all this is not at all a matter of abstract theory. The grace of God shines out in the faces of his servants. Sibbald himself has seen it.

In a striking passage at the end of the sermon where Sibbald speaks directly of Patrick Forbes, he describes the way in which the Bishop's speech was impressive on account not only of his eloquence but also of his facial expression. 'His face and eyes (as ye know) were shining; so that by his speech things were presented rather to the sight than conveyed to the ear.' [21] In an age which prized hearing as much as the seventeenth century did, this is a very striking assertion. The radiance of the inner man as it were 'broke out' into the outward appearance of the speaker, so that in him, the simple act of reading the Scripture aloud, conveyed more than much study of commentaries or expositions would have done.

It is against the background of such a doctrine of the creation and restoration of man, and of the part which man has to play in this drama, that we must read the affirmations which Sibbald makes about the scope and nature of the Christian ministry at the end of this sermon, for it is here that he may surprise us most by his whole-hearted and complete acceptance of the patristic view of priesthood. These are not just extreme statements of ministerial prerogatives, nor are they primarily polemical in intention. They are an integral part of a vision of man's life as capable of becoming divine, an integral part of a vision of Christianity which Sibbald felt he had seen embodied in the particular flesh and blood of the man who in 1618 when Laird of Corse, had reluctantly accepted to become Bishop of Aberdeen.

To express this Sibbald turns again to Chrysostom, quoting passages which were much loved and used by his English contemporaries, George Herbert and Jeremy Taylor.

Though all God's people should 'worship him in the beauty of holiness', yet more especially they that serve at the Lord's altar. . . . Their office requireth a particular sanctification inward, by the grace of God's Spirit, working an ardent and fervent desire of hallowing the Name of God; giving power and skill to dispense the means of holiness, and moving them to go before others in a life exemplarily holy; a particular sanctification outward by the authority of the Church, separating and consecrating them with prayers, supplications, and imposition of hands, to this sacred office, to be fellow-workers with God, and his instrument in sanctifying and saving man. . . . 'Priesthood' saith Chrysostom in his excellent Books *De Sacerdotio, Lib 3*, 'is performed on earth; but yet it is to be counted in the rank of heavenly things'. And therefore a priest must be so pure, as if in heaven itself he were walking among heavenly powers. Terrible were those things which preceded the time of grace, as bells, pomegranets, precious stones, the mitre, the plate of gold, the Holiest of Holies, etc. Yet, saith he, if we compare them with the things that are under the time of grace, we will find them to be very light; and that true which St Paul saith, II Cor. 3 – 'For while thou beholdest the Lord sacrificed, the priest performing that sacrifice pouring out prayers, and the people died, as it were, and made red with that precious blood, thinkest thou that thou art yet amongst mortal men, and on the earth? Art thou not rather translated to heaven? . . .' And *Lib. 6* he saith to the same purpose, when the priest performeth this most sublime part of Christian service in the Eucharist – 'I demand', saith he, 'where shall we rank him? What integrity should we require of him? What religion? How innocent should those hands be that serve? How pure the tongue that uttereth those words? What things should be so pure and clean as the soul that receiveth so great and worthy a Spirit?' 'At that time', saith he, 'the angels stand beside, and the whole order of the heavenly powers do shout.' 'What is required of him', saith Nazianzen, 'that is to stand with the angels, and to praise with the archangels, and send sacrifice to the altar that is above, and to discharge priesthood with Christ, and to restore the frame of mankind, and to renew his image, and to be an architect for that superior world; and to say more, Θεόν ἐσόμενον και θεοποιήσαντα, who becometh

74

himself God and maketh others such?'. . . Therefore, whereas all Christians should be and are called *sancti*, holy, Christian bishops should be, and have been styled *sanctissimi*, most holy.[22]

In a recent study of the Christian tradition, *Summer in the Seed*, Aelred Squire has pointed to the way in which the doctrine of *theosis*, deification, which held such a central place in the teaching of the Church during the first twelve centuries, has come to be more and more neglected in the West.[23] Indeed in most Catholic and Protestant theology it continues today to be in eclipse. Much has been said about that from which man must be saved, much about the way in which salvation takes place. The actual content of that salvation, that for which man was created in the beginning, has been less insisted on. The courage of the earlier centuries in speaking of the reconciliation of man with God in terms of the taking up of human life in its totality into union with the divine has no longer been in evidence. Something of that holy boldness, that freedom of access into the deep things of God, of which St Paul speaks and which St John presupposes, has been lost to sight. At times indeed the whole character of the Christian religion seems to be reversed. What begins as a transcendent affirmation of life – human and divine – 'I am come that they might have life and have it in abundance' – becomes instead negative, self-regarding, anxious, destructive of life and joy.

What is striking in the teaching of these scholars of Aberdeen is that this doctrine is so strongly and explicitly present. It shows us something of the central affirmation by which their understanding of the faith was controlled. It is one of the many factors which links their work with that of some of their English contemporaries. Lancelot Andrewes is no less outspoken on the subject. Their common affirmation of this point illustrates in a vivid way the meaning of Andrewes' prayer 'for the whole Church, Eastern, Western, and our own'. It is a testimony to a sense of catholicity in time, as well as in space, a sense of catholicity which is as much a question of wholeness of vision as it is of universal extension. All this is the more striking in that Sibbald, like Andrewes, was living in a world in which it was impossible to ignore the schisms caused by the Reformation, schisms which were about to multiply again. All this he does not seek to evade. Rather through the discontin-

75

uities of which he must be aware, through the divisions which he seeks to remedy, he manages to affirm a deeper and more inclusive, underlying unity.

So in St Nicholas' Church in Aberdeen, the years are overpast. The mysteries made known in Galilee and Judaea, experienced again with such vividness in Antioch and Constantinople, in Hippo and Milan, communicate themselves afresh in seventeenth century Scotland. There is a remarkable wholeness of vision here, a surprising conjunction of Christian East and West. The human dimensions of the life of Patrick Forbes, his sense of justice and equity, his gifts of conciliation and understanding, his evident sense of what was practicable and possible in the difficult circumstances of his time and place, all these are seen as rooted in a Godward dimension of prayer and faith and love, a dimension in which man is lifted up in union with the divine. The holiness which is in God, which is a power which draws men together into life and unity, is seen at work in God's minister, who thus becomes in fact and not just in title a father in God, one who receives life and transmits it. In him the tradition is recapitulated, and becomes present; the remote and apparently inaccessible past is laid open to us.

It was a remarkable moment in Aberdeen. The vision and capacity of men like Bishops Elphinstone and Dunbar, which at the end of the Middle Ages had compassed the re-building of the Cathedral and the foundation of the University, was seen again a century and a half later, in the altered circumstances of the seventeenth century. Within five years of his death the whole work which Patrick Forbes had fostered and built up was being cast down in the passions and conflicts of the Civil War. The doctors were silenced and dispersed, since none of them felt able to subscribe the National Covenant. Their hopes and aspirations were apparently dashed for ever. John Forbes is without a monument or any known grave. The end of Little Gidding in England seemed equally decisive. 'Mid-winter spring is its own season.' Certainly in Aberdeen some memory of this episode lingered on into the eighteenth century. It is not by chance that in 1784, the first bishop of the American Episcopal Church was consecrated, not in London or in Canterbury, but in Aberdeen. In the economy of God, such times and places are not forgotten, do not lose their power and meaning. Is there in this short but brilliant episode in the spiritual and intellectual history of Scotland, a message of hope for a Christendom which still seeks the renewal of its unity, which still looks for a tradition which is life-giving? Surely there are universal meanings here which have yet to be explored.

Chapter 4

The Liberating Power of Praise

In the previous chapters we have been considering two moments in the English-speaking history of the island of Britain which seem to have a surprising importance at the present time, moments which are making their presence felt in our own century, and which themselves contain a richness of inheritance from the past.

We now turn to the hidden side of the heritage of Britain and speak of the Celtic tradition in our island, a tradition whose present condition is humanly-speaking fragile and precarious, indeed, whose very existence is scarcely recognized, but whose significance for our present and our future is, I believe, very great. We shall be concerned almost entirely with the Welsh element in this tradition, and shall try to see something of its own particular sense of the presence of the past, and of the surprising continuity of its literary tradition.

In a steep valley of North-East Wales, not very far from the English border at Llandysilio-yn-Iâl, there stands a stone known as the Elisedd pillar. The monument as we now see it is only half its original height. Originally it had the form of a great standing cross; it has given its name to the nearby Cistercian abbey, Valle Crucis. The inscription on the monument is almost wholly illegible. What we know of it we have from a transcript made by the pioneering Celtic scholar, Edward Lhuyd in 1696. Easy neither of access nor of interpretation, the pillar might act as a parable for the monuments of the early history of Wales. It is easy to overlook them. But here is a historical document of unrivalled interest.

From the inscription we learn that the monument was erected

by Cyngen, King of Powys, the kingdom in mid-Wales which confronted the English advance across Offa's dyke. Cyngen's reign, which was a long one, extended over a large part of the first half of the ninth century. He died an old man when on pilgrimage to Rome in 854. He erected the monument in the first place to the memory of his great-grandfather Elisedd who had flourished just over a century before. Elisedd had enlarged and established his kingdom over against the English, and Cyngen himself had followed in his footsteps. The monument then takes us back to the origins of their dynasty. It refers to the late fourth century Emperor Magnus Maximus and to King Vortigern the British king in the first part of the following century. Legend says that it was he who invited the Anglo-Saxon invaders into Kent, but this inscription remembers him as having been blessed by St Germanus of Auxerre. The two visits of Germanus to this country in 429 and 447 respectively are among the best attested facts from this extremely obscure period in our history. The inscription ends with these lines: '*Conmarch pinxit hoc chirographum, rege suo poscente Concenn*,' 'Conmarch (or Cynfarch) painted this inscription at the demand of his king Cyngen'. '*Benedictio Dñi in Concenn et Suos in tota familia eius, et in totam regionen Pouis usque in diem Iudicii. Amen,*' 'The blessing of God be upon Cyngen and those of his family and on the whole land of Powys until the day of judgement.'

The monument is in many ways a remarkable one. Nash-Williams in his indispensable work *The Early Christian Monuments of Wales*, remarks that it is 'probably the most elaborate record of its kind surviving from the Early Christian period in Britain.' [1] It shows us a king proud of his own achievement and that of his immediate ancestors in stemming the advance of the English invaders. It speaks for a society which is conscious of its Latin Christian culture, which recalls its links with the Imperial government before the Empire had to withdraw from Britain, and its connections with the leaders of the Church, who provided one of the elements of continuity through that period of upheaval and destruction. Both in its form and its content the monument speaks of this Roman and Christian heritage, and it is not altogether surprising that its author should have died in the city of the Apostles. Pilgrimage to Rome was something shared by rulers both of Welsh and Anglo-Saxon Britain at this time. Alfred was there as a boy only one year before the death of Cyngen. It is tantalizing to think that the young prince of Wessex and the ageing ruler of Powys might have met in the streets of Rome. The rather strange way in which, at the end, the sculptor speaks of himself 'Cynfarch painted this inscription (chirographum)' may possibly reflect the priorities of the Celtic world in which it was erected, and relate to the prestige and renown of the illuminated manuscripts which are amongst the finest products of the meeting of cultures in the North. This, at least, is Nash-Williams' suggestion. But it could also be that the word 'chirographum' reflects the established usage of a royal curia. In either case the inscription speaks of a sophisticated if materially fragile society.

The Elisedd Pillar has no equal as a stone monument. But what it tells us of the society which created it, is confirmed by all that we know of the earliest Welsh poetry. It is now generally agreed that the compositions of the two first Welsh poets, Aneirin and Taliesin date from the end of the sixth century. The poems of Taliesin celebrate the victories and the conflicts of the rulers of Rheged, what is now the southern part of Scotland, and it has been argued that they represent a literature which was aware of its Virgilian heritage. We may remark in parenthesis on the startling insight contained in Charles Williams' poem on the battle of Badon. Anachronistically, Williams has made 'Taliessin' court poet to Arthur, more than fifty years earlier than the historical Taliesin's life. But the point of the poem turns not on this question of detail but on the idea of the past as informing the present. Taliesin has charge of a troop of cavalry at the battle of Badon. His hesitations about where precisely to engage in the battle are resolved by a vision of Virgil, centuries before, suddenly finding the word that he needs for a hexameter. The disciplined art of the poet inspires and enables the disciplined art of the military commander. Barbarian chaos is, for a moment, held back:

The grand art mastered the thudding hammer of Thor,
And the heart of our Lord Taliessin determined the war.[2]

The strange thing is that Williams can hardly have known that his vision of the relationship between Taliesin and Virgil could have had any historical basis, since the results of the research which are now available to us had not then been published.

This literary tradition which emerges in the sixth century, continues to this day. One of its most striking characteristics is its astonishing sense of continuity through time. The practice of singing the praise of kings and warriors continued for at least another seven centuries after the time of Taliesin. When after the death of Llywelyn the Last, in 1282, the last independent Welsh princedom was destroyed, the poetic tradition took another turn and emerged in the fourteenth century into the most brilliant and creative period of its entire history. Even through the period of decline which followed the Acts of Union in the sixteenth century which prohibited the use of the Welsh language in law and administration this tradition never died out. One can find a leading representative of Calvinistic Methodism in the first years of the nineteenth century, Thomas Jones of Denbigh, writing an ode to a thrush, in the style and manner of the masters of the fifteenth century.[3] Saunders Lewis gives as another example, a poem of congratulation written to a squire in South-West Wales on the launching of his ship in 1771. The poem, the work of an otherwise unknown local poet, reflects the whole history of Welsh literature. 'We cannot pluck a flower of song off a headland in Dyfed in the late eighteenth century without stirring a great northern star of the sixth century. And all the intermediaries are involved. The fourteenth century gave the technique of *dyfalu* or image-making, the sixteenth century brought in the Virgilian echoes, the seventeenth century gave the measure. The whole body of Welsh poetry from the sixth century onwards has contributed directly to Ioan Siencyn's verses.'[4]

In our own day this poetic tradition has known yet another revival. The Welsh language poets of the twentieth century have been many and distinguished. In a great variety of ways their work reveals something of the astonishing vitality of a line of writers which began almost fourteen hundred years ago. Everything which Eliot says in his essay, about the poet as one who senses the presence, as well as the pastness of the past, who finds himself to be part of a simultaneous order which includes the whole literature of his country, who sees that the historical sense involves an awareness of the timeless and the temporal together, all this is eminently true of the Welsh tradition, true in a way which cannot always be matched in other literatures which have been less marked by this constant concern to recapitulate and remember what has gone before. In particular in the poetry of the last forty years one has a totally unexpected way of access to a far earlier period of the Christian tradition, the formative period marked by the Elisedd pillar.

How is one to account for this phenomenon? It is a large question which admits of many answers. It is a question particularly difficult to resolve from outside, since so very little is known of the subject beyond the boundaries of Welsh-speaking Wales, the English having adhered faithfully to their resolve, now fifteen centuries old, not to learn the language of their Western neighbours. And here we must pause to consider something of the significance of this fact, which were it not so familar, we might recognize as somehow curiously painful and sad. For fifteen hundred years the English and Welsh languages have lived side by side, in very close proximity. It is true that for much the greater part of this time English has been the dominant partner. Signs of this fact are very evident at the level of language. English loan words are common in Welsh. Welsh loan-words in English are very few. Thus while the relationship between our two cultures and peoples has been very close, on the English side it has been almost wholly unconscious. The classics of Welsh literature, with the partial exception of the *Mabinogion* remain virtually unknown to readers throughout the English-speaking world. The study of the Welsh language is regarded as a highly specialized pursuit, undertaken in very few universities in England, let alone in the United States, Canada, Australia or New Zealand. To what a degree this implies impoverishment for those whose mother tongue is English may at least be suggested by the contents of this chapter. To be ignorant of Welsh is to be ignorant of much that throws light on the origins and development of the whole tradition of Britain. To discover the world of Wales is like finding hidden rooms in an ancient house with which one thought one had long been familiar. There are things which need investigation here, particularly if we think it is important for a people to be aware of their roots.

There are however two facts about contemporary Welsh life and culture which are at least vaguely known to many English people. First there is an annual folk festival known as the national Eisteddfod. Secondly there is the continuing prevalence of popular hymn-singing, a practice which even more than in England shows an astonishing resilience in face of increasing secularization. Let us then start from these two points, the popular nature of Welsh culture as suggested by the Eisteddfod, and the strength of the Christian element within it.

As we have suggested in earlier chapters, the practice of prayer and praise creates unexpected links across the separations of time as well as the separations of space. Praise, not only of the princes, of beautiful women and of nature, but above all praise of God, has throughout been at the heart of the Welsh tradition. And the line of poets which began in the age of the saints, that moment when in Wales as well as in Ireland, the Christian West produced a monastic flowering to rival that of Palestine and Egypt, was supported in a later century by the prayer of the Cistercian revival, which had a particularly strong influence in Wales, and at a crucial moment in the twelfth and thirteenth centuries provided an element of continuity in a time of upheaval and disaster. This same tradition of prayer and praise blossomed again in a different form in the time of the Methodist revival of the eighteenth century, the period at which the greatest hymns were written. It may be that it is the overarching and unifying presence of prayer, and the liberating power of praise which have been the deepest cause of this sense of a living communion across the ages, which marks the Welsh tradition so deeply.

We have said that we shall start from the Eisteddfod, the *National* as it is known in Wales, to distinguish it from all the other smaller examples of the same species. Here is an event which annually brings together more than fifty thousand people, more than one in ten of the Welsh-speaking population of Wales. What does the observer see at it? A great deal of singing, a great deal of public speaking, the reading and adjudication of poetry and the reading and adjudication of prose. All this is accompanied by certain rather strange druidic-looking ceremonies, for the most devised by an eccentric antiquarian at the end of the eighteenth century. But here is the central national institution, until recent years almost the only national institution, of a people which has preserved its sense of identity, not through its legal, administrative, or financial organizations – for centuries it has had none – but through the use of a language which at a great variety of levels from the most popular and unthinking, to the most sophisticated and scientific, in forms both secular and religious, has carried with it a practice of speech and song, of poetry and declamation which has coloured the whole life of the people.

How can it be that poetry and speech can be so powerful in the maintenance of the identity of a nation? For a society like ours in England where these activities are for the most part regarded as marginal and purely decorative, the preserve of a small elite, it is difficult to understand. We need to go to Eastern Europe to find other nations where poetry can be a public, powerful and at times subversive activity, where the national language conveys in a particular way the whole national heritage. Listen to the Bishops of Poland in their Pastoral Letter of May 1978 on 'The Duties of Polish Catholics towards their National and Religious Culture', a document in which we can surely hear the voice of Pope John Paul: 'The cultivation of speech and language is the strongest spiritual bond which links each one of us with the national community, with the community of our native land. Those who are aware of the importance of this link, at home as well as in the emigration, have always taken to heart the need to defend the purity of the mother tongue and its zone of influence. This is verified by our national experience both in the time of slavery, and in the time of dispersion and emigration.' [5] The letter is a fine exposition of the way in which each nation is called to be true to the whole of its heritage, and by being true to its own heritage is enabled to make its specific contribution to mankind as a whole.

But there is more involved here than the question of the preservation of a national identity and a national experience. Behind these words there lie convictions about the way in which language and speech, poetry and music, shape and increase our possibilities of life both personal and social. It is not simply a question of aesthetic satisfaction. Words, especially when they are given power by song, create in us new capacities both for action and for understanding. The Orthodox Church with its wealth of poetic texts, texts which are always chanted or sung in its fervent liturgical celebration, knows this very well. Let us hear another voice from Eastern Europe, Fr Dumitru Staniloae, the most distinguished of Romanian theologians, speaking of the power of the liturgy to create new capacities in those who participate in it: 'The amazing spiritual beauty of God and of the life which participates in him cannot be fully apprehended within the boundaries which are determined by the meaning of words. These inexplicable riches are more fully expressed in music which overflows through the meanings which the words define. . . . Song unites men's minds, making them commune with one another beyond every definition, and unifying them in endless and life-giving joy, in a way beyond that which words with their defined and distinct meanings, which divide and limit, are able to do; and thus men's lives are strengthened in their good resolutions by each other and by God who is the source of this endless and life-giving joy. The melody makes the meaning of the words shared and loved, the words themselves being the dynamic basis of the infinite richness of meanings which are expressed through the melody. Thus a communion or common identity is created in the worshipping congregation.' [6] Anyone who has heard or, still better, shared in Welsh hymn-singing knows something of what is meant. We may surely reflect that if a theology of this kind had been more widely influential in the West, we should have been better equipped to understand and guide the movements of religious enthusiasm which have marked our recent centuries.

In another passage where he is commenting on the exposition of the liturgy, written in the seventh century by Maximus the Confessor, Fr Staniloae concludes:

We see in all this how St Maximus always links action and knowledge with the enthusiasm which becomes hymnody. Song enlarges the active and intellectual powers of man, widening the horizons of what is known and what can be known. On the other hand, possibilities which are realized in action, horizons of reality which are opened to the mind, increase the enthusiasm of the soul. There are possibilities of action and knowledge latent in joy. And there are possibilities of joy in those good acts which truly develop reality, and in our coming to know that reality. The good and true reality is joyful. [7]

Here is an understanding of speech and song, especially of sacred speech and song, which throws light on the whole Celtic tradition in its many different forms, secular as well as religious. As in most early cultures the bards chanted or sang their poems. And the songs of praise to the prince and his warriors, were ultimately rooted in songs of praise to God. The way in which melody can widen and enlarge the meaning of words sung, by adding to the meanings which the words express directly, resonances and meanings which can only be suggested, applies *mutatis mutandis* to the poetic art itself, where the task of the poet is to restore to words their original fulness of meaning and association. This is particularly true for those kinds of poetry which approach most closely to music, as is the case throughout the classical Welsh tradition. The very word for poetry, *Cerdd Dafod*, (tongue-craft), as opposed to *Cerdd Dant* (string-craft, i.e. music) is significant in this regard. We see here something of the meaning of the medieval Welsh conviction that a poem yields its sweetness to the ear, and from the ear to the heart. The heart here is not to be understood simply as the seat of the emotions, but, as in the Bible and the liturgy, as that centre in man from which his thoughts and decisions no less than his longings and aspirations originate. The meaning of a poem strikes home to the heart, for the time at least by-passing the analytical intellect. Only later do we find it helpful to examine it in detail, to take it to pieces and tease out its complexities, and in doing so to realize something of the labour, the skill, the craftsmanship which went into the making of this apparently effortless work.

Let us come directly to the hymns of the Methodist revival. They are the product of the eighteenth and nineteenth centuries, and in some ways they seem not to belong to the mainstream of the Welsh poetic tradition. There are differences both in form and content. The complexities of metrical form which are characteristic of the earlier centuries are abandoned for simple, popular metres, often borrowed from the English hymnwriting of the same period. When we come to what is said, we find that the sense that the praise of God is to be celebrated in and through the praise of all that he has made, gives way to an apparently world-denying attitude, in which the singer turns his back on creation in order to contemplate the beauties of God. And this tension between the world and God has remained a constant feature of the life of Welsh non-conformity and has been deeply felt in the poetry of the last forty years, which has been a period of an extraordinary flowering of Christian verse. It has, we may discover, been resolved in a remarkable way, but not without struggle.

What are we to say to all this? First we must remark on the fact that the content of the hymns is often of a remarkable quality in terms of the Christian tradition as a whole. They contain theological and dogmatic affirmations of classical clarity and balance. This is particularly the case with the hymns of Ann Griffiths, in whose verse the great paradoxes which characterize the hymns of the Byzantine epoch (with which she can have had no direct acquaintance) come to life again at the beginning of the nineteenth century in Wales in a way which astonishes us.[8] The same is true, in a similar way, of the hymns of Williams Pantycelyn, by far the greatest of the writers of this school. In him too there is an objective content of faith, in even the most passionately felt of his verses. We are not dealing here with the sentimental self-concern of a good deal of more recent hymn-writing. We are in touch with works at once dogmatic and ecstatic, which make accessible to the ordinary people of the Church, some of the deepest mysteries of the faith. Let us take an example from a writer of the second rank, a hymn still well known and loved:

Great was Christ in heavenly glory,
Great when man he came to save;
Great his wondrous incarnation,
Death and victory o'er the grave.
King today, 'neath his sway,
Heaven and earth their homage pay.

(Mawr oedd Crist yn nhragwyddoldeb,
Mawr yn gwisgo natur dyn;
Mawr yn marw ar Galfaria,
Mawr yn maeddu angau'i hun;
Hynod fawr yw yn awr,
Brenin nef a daear lawr.)

Great is Jesus in his Person;
Great as God and great as man;
Great his comeliness and beauty,
Radiance of the Father's plan.
All shall see, great is he,
King through all eternity.

(Mawr yw Iesu yn ei Berson;
Mawr fel Duw, a mawr fel dyn;

Mawr ei degwch a'i hawddgarwch,
Gwyn a gwridog, teg ei lun:
Mawr yw Ef yn y nef
Ar ei orsedd gadarn gref.)[9]

When a congregation is caught up into verses such as these we are aware that the meaning of the affirmation of Christ's sovereignty is being illuminated for us in something like the same way that it is by the mosaic of *Christ Pantocrator* in the dome of a Byzantine church. Nothing in earlier Welsh tradition had begun to equal this as an affirmation, at once popular and articulate, of the Christian faith. The liturgy had been there, of course, in its Latin form before the Reformation, and in the stately Welsh of the Book of Common Prayer in the centuries that followed. But here was a new and original creation. If there are vital elements of liturgy lacking in the worship of Welsh Protestantism, the hymns do much to compensate for the things that are missing. Doubtless to understand the quality of this way of worship we should have to examine the history of preaching, itself constantly dogmatic-ecstatic, but that would take us far beyond the bounds of this chapter.

Secondly, it is true we need to recognize that while in the earlier Welsh tradition the praise of men and animals, of birds and the natural order was rooted ultimately in the praise of God, poets themselves were not unconscious that there could be a tension between the praise of God and the praise of the world. Men and women could be flattered for every kind of motive, sometimes of the basest kind. Can such praise be reconciled with the praise of God? This tension is particularly evident in the case of Dafydd ap Gwilym, the greatest of the medieval poets, with his anti-clerical gibes and his celebration of illicit love. Some recent critics indeed have maintained that the poetry of the fourteenth and fifteenth centuries is essentially secular, and simply coloured at times with Christian imagery which forms an incongruous element in works which are basically pagan and mundane. Can we accept such a line of argument? Is it true that the Christian faith, if we take it seriously, demands that we should turn our backs on the beauties of this world? Is the praise of God in the end incompatible with the praise of his creatures?

To this there can be only one answer from the side of Christianity. All things that are, come from God; they are his creation and he is to be praised in and for them, and they are to be praised as his gifts to us, full of his glory. And if through the fall of man it has become impossible for us to see them in this way, Christ through his redemptive incarnation has again made clear that all things hold together in him, and that in him all things are known by God as very good. The tendency to suggest that this world in its specificity and earthiness, in its materiality and multiplicity is bad, or at least irrelevant to our approach to God, is less than Christian. It has invaded Christianity from time to time. We see it in some strands of the early monastic movement, though not in that movement as a whole; we see it in some strands of the evangelical and puritan movements in Wales no less than elsewhere, though not in that movement at its best. In both cases it represents a deviation from the norm. What is true from the point of view of the Christian tradition is that unless we are willing to turn away for a time from the world we may never truly find the world again as God's world. Only by recognizing the Creator as greater than his creation can we again come to see the creation as his gift to us, full of the goodness of the Giver. In this sense the movement of renunciation is a necessary step on the way towards God. It is not the whole of the way.[10]

Here again the position of Eastern Orthodoxy is very illuminating. To quote again from Fr Staniloae commenting on the work of St Maximus, the man who already in this life has arrived at some true experience and vision of God, does not thereby become indifferent to the things of this world, 'he loves all things and all men in God. He does not wish to possess or to love this or that object in a state of separation, but in union with God. Knowing God he knows him as All in all things and all people. He knows him as "All", since there exists nothing in anything which does not belong to God; "in all things and all people," because such a man does not live the experience of God in each separated object by itself, but in its connection with all things and all people. He sees every particular thing linked with all other things, and he sees God only in his relationship with all things. He has this experience while he is still living in the body. For his body is not separate from his link with all things.' Indeed, in the Orthodox tradition it is essential to say that we approach God with the whole of ourselves, with the body and the senses, no less than with the mind and the imagination. 'Consequently one can say that it is not matter as matter which is a hindrance to the vision of God, but its opaqueness, caused by men's passionate attachment to it.'[11]

One of the most striking qualities of the Christian poetry of Wales of the last forty years has been the way in which it has succeeded in conveying again, in our late and unpropitious times this very same vision, the sense of a transfigured world which is so clearly to be seen in the work of some of the earlier centuries. In response to the life-denying element in later Methodism, Gwenallt can affirm:

God has not forbidden us to love the world
And to love man and all his works,
To love it with all the naked senses together
Every shape and colour, every voice and every sound.
There is a shudder in our blood when we see
The traces of his craftsman's hands upon the world . . .[12]

And Euros Bowen, in a poem which begins with a reference to a line from Ann Griffiths, 'What have I to do any longer with the base idols of earth?' replies:

But to compare,
beauty
and delight
and majesty
with the poetry
inspired
by the poor idols of the world.[13]

The poet sees all things in their own specific natures, but in all of them he sees as Euros says, 'elements of goodness', *y daioni*, the creative power and wisdom of God which flows through all things.

To see things in this way there is a certain renunciation which is necessary. We have to abandon the attempt to possess and exploit, to hold on to things and use them for our own purposes, if we are again to see them as transparent to the light. Those Irish lyrics of the tenth century which so wonderfully express delight in the song of a bird, or the sound of a brook, came from men living a life of great renunciation. *The Canticle of the Creatures* was written when St Francis was almost blind. But turning to God we find all things given back by him.

Such acts of praise are then full of a liberating and purifying power. Dr Bobi Jones in his recent study of the religious element in Welsh literature, *Llên Cymru a Chrefydd*, having considered the purposes of praise in primitive societies, concludes:

> Praise, all praise, is a positive response to the purpose of life, and there is a way in which praise to God, to Urien, to Morfudd, or to the lark contributes to the purposes of each and to their relationship to one another. But when it comes to the praise of God, the meanings of all the other forms of praise are gathered into one ultimate point. The only reason to praise God is not in order to benefit man (though to praise God does, in fact, benefit him) nor of course to benefit God, but simply because it was for this that man was created. Man is not complete until he glorifies God, in word and in deed. The most sound, the most complete, the most joyful thing that he can do is to praise God.[14]

There speaks the scholar, the poet, and the believer in one. In all things God is to be praised. The poets of the Middle Ages see all things held together by the creative power of God the Maker of all. They see the world as God's world, grace and nature at every point interpenetrating and supporting one another. And this the writers of Wales have done again for us, even in our own generation, in a great variety of ways, speaking together but with highly individual voices.

Thus we have the unlooked for fact that in the writers of Wales in the last forty years something of the original vision of the age of the saints has been made accessible to us in its fulness and balance. We have a magnificent expression of that plenitude of faith and understanding which characterized the teaching of the Church in the centuries before the schism of East and West. Something of that proportion and perspective which we find in the Fathers of these earlier centuries, and which was so powerfully present in the early period of Celtic Christianity, has come to birth at this late moment in the history of the West. Something of the quality which we see in France, for instance, in a poet like Charles Péguy, the holding together in one of the things of earth and the things of heaven, the transfiguration of the world of flesh and matter, is to be found here too. If there is place for renunciation, there is beyond it a further place for thanksgiving and praise.

We may seem in this discussion of the relationship between the two ways of affirmation and negation to have strayed rather far from our original theme of the element of continuity in the Welsh tradition as seen in its popular and religious character. What I have hoped to show is that the Methodist movement of the eighteenth century, which in some ways might be taken to indicate a break in that tradition, has in the end proved to be a source of its enrichment. Through the break and all that followed from it, the tradition has been reaffirmed, with a new power and a new awareness.

We can see this in the work of many writers of our own century. For instance in Gwenallt's beautiful lyric in which he praises God that the dust of the saints of all the ages has made the land holy, and that the light of God's grace has touched the life of his people at every point.[15] We can see it in the poetry of Euros Bowen, from whom we have already quoted. Indeed in some ways the work of this writer, who follows an explicitly sacramental path in the whole of his poetic work, gives us the most concentrated expression of this tradition. In one particular poem *Golau*, *Light*, Euros recapitulates the history of Welsh verse, finding in it sources of constant inner renewal through apparent outer defeat. He finds that through all the years, as he says at the end of another poem:

The power of song shall purify woe.[16]

But the last words should be with Saunders Lewis, the greatest and most influential figure in Welsh-speaking Wales in our century. In his poem on 'The Last Sermon of St David', he meditates on the way in which the last words of the saint, 'Be joyful, keep the faith, and do the little things you heard and saw from me' may have been preserved in unwritten tradition through the ages, till many centuries later they were consigned to writing by the anchorite at Llanddewi Brefi:

And it may be that it was from the recollection in the
memories of rustic believers
Who had wandered the banks of the Teifi like prayers
Slipping one by one through the fingers of the centuries

That the version the anchorite put in his parchment was
found. . . .

It is in the 'little things', the repetitive tasks of farm and household
that, through the centuries, men and women have been faithful to
that vision; not apart from, but in and through the materiality of
daily life. And, through it all, it has been the overarching and
unifying presence of prayer, the liberating power of praise, which
has kept alive the tradition through the centuries, and has linked
the generations together in the communion of a life which transcends the barriers of time and space. 'There is a continuity of
Presence, which is creative and life-giving at every moment – one
could say a contemporaneity of the Spirit.' As we have seen before
the saints of different times and places come together in unexpected,
unlooked for ways. Communion in the life of God reveals unexpected likenesses across the centuries. It is the point Mr Lewis
makes at the end of his poem. It was not the legendary severity of
St David which remained in people's minds:

But his last words, the sermon that nestled in the memories
Of those who prayed on the banks of the Teifi through
centuries
Of terror, through war, under the scowl of the vulture castles,
Through the ages when the grasshopper was a burden.
They are the words of a maiden, the gentleness of a nun,
The 'little way' of St Therese towards the purification and the
union
And the way of the poor maid who saw Mary at Lourdes.[17]

As David Jones remarks in one of his later essays, there are
perhaps no shrines in Wales, because Wales itself is a shrine.[18] And
this is not the calling of one country alone, but of all, for all are
called to be places of God, temples of the one Spirit.

Chapter 5

The Sense of the Whole

In the last three chapters we have been considering our subject with the aid of examples taken from crucial moments in the history of the island of Britain. We have tried to see what 'the intersection of the timeless with time' implies in particular cases, some well known, some very little known. Our method has been to a large extent historical. Now, without altogether abandoning this appeal to the past, which is an inherent part of what we are trying to do, we shall consider the question more in relation to the present and the future, and more directly in relation to that which is eternal, which though it reveals itself in time is yet beyond time. For as we said at the beginning, our concern with the past was not cold and detached. While at all costs we must avoid reading into the past simply what we want to see there, I believe we shall see very little, at least in the fields which we are considering here, unless we realize that we are ourselves involved. The past of man touches us directly. It is as we are truly able to recollect and remember it that we become able to live fully in the present, creatively towards the future.

In the passage from Eliot with which we began, he spoke not only of the need to be aware of the timeless as well as the temporal, but also of the need for the writer to be conscious of an inclusive and simultaneous order, 'the whole literature of Europe from Homer until today'. In the last chapter we thought of the literature of Wales in that way, and we were dealing with the literature of a small country which, partly because it has lived under strong external pressures, has maintained an unusually vivid sense of inner coherence and unity. To see such a unity in the literature of England, let alone of Europe as a whole would be less easy, but not for that reason less important. To see such a unity not in a literary tradition alone, but in that of a whole religion may be still more challenging, but still more worthwhile.

In his later essay 'What is a Classic?' Eliot takes up the question again in relation to the place of Virgil within the Latin tradition, and to his significance for us today. 'The Roman Empire and the Latin language were not any empire and any language, but an empire and a language with a unique destiny in relation to ourselves; and the poet in whom that empire and that language came to consciousness and expression is a poet of unique destiny.' [1] Here even more than in the earlier essay, Eliot is concerned with the danger that we shall get cut off from the past, confined within a temporal provincialism. 'In our age, when men seem more than ever to confuse wisdom with knowledge, and knowledge with information, and try to solve the problem of life in terms of engineering, there is coming into existence a new kind of provincialism, which perhaps deserves a new name. It is a provincialism not of space, but of time; one for which history is merely the chronicle of human devices which have served their turn and been scrapped, one for which the world is the property solely of the living, a property in which the dead hold no shares. [And surely, we might add, in view of the unthinking way in which we use up the earth's material resources, in which the unborn hold no shares either.] The menace of this kind of provincialism is, that we can all, all the peoples of the globe, be provincials together; and those who are not content to become provincials can only become hermits.' [2] It is this kind of provincialism which has in theological terms been stigmatized by David Jenkins, when he speaks of the tendency to ignore the whole experience of the people of God from the time of Abraham to Schleiermacher.[3] It is against this tendency that Fr George Florovsky, perhaps the greatest Orthodox scholar of our time, spoke in stressing the necessity for an ecumenism in time as well as in space.

But it must be confessed that Eliot himself, in that essay, with his rather static definition of a classic and his insistence on the Latin element in our inheritance, seems himself, at least from a standpoint of a generation later, to have become a little provincial. In his poetry he had shown himself more wide ranging. There we find references not only to Greece and Rome and to the Judaeo-Christian inheritance, but also to the Buddha, to the Upanishads and the Bhagavad-Gita. And what might have been regarded as perhaps somewhat esoteric fifty years ago, has come much closer to us now. The presence of the civilizations and the religions which had little or no connection with the old world of Christendom has become much more generally and much more strongly felt. Christian theology in the future will not be able to develop credibly, unless it takes into account, with a wholly new seriousness, the presence and the witness of the great world religions.

But before we come to consider that question, let us first think a little more of what is involved in escaping from the kind of provincialism within the Christian world which is likely to afflict us. Here we come across one of the most important, though least understood aspects of the movement towards Christian unity. This is the recovery of a wholeness of vision, the rediscovery of the Christian tradition in its integrity, that ecumenism in time which means that we no longer need be cut off from large parts of our inheritance, but have access to all. Here too we find one of the most vital but least regarded elements in this movement, its doctrinal basis. Growth in Christian unity does not come about by everyone sitting lightly to their own fundamental convictions, and gradually adopting an attitude of relativism. During the last sixty years this convergence has developed around the rediscovery and the reaffirmation of the great central doctrines of the Trinity and the Incarnation, and around a new discernment of how those central articles of the faith can be distinguished from ulterior theological developments, which, however important they may be, need always to be referred back to these fundamental articles. It is in these subsequent developments that most of the divisions and controversies have taken place. There has been at the heart of all the major Christian traditions an almost unnoticed accord on what is most essential. The recovery of a living sense of the presence and power of God, Three in One, in the midst of his people is the starting point from which the movement towards unity can set out. It reveals to us how much we already share across the apparently widest gulfs within the Christian family.

All this is by no means only a matter for theological and historical experts, though they have their part to play in it. It may well be, as Thomas Merton describes it, the achievement of a type of inner Catholicity through the reconciliation within ourselves of different elements within the Christian tradition. It may be, much more simply, the discovery of a saint, a book, an icon from some other part of the Christian world which suddenly we find to be intimately linked with us; the meeting with someone far away in space and time who yet becomes our friend and our contemporary.

The basic conviction from which such an enterprise must begin is the truth of the words *Non vos relinquam orphanos*, I will not leave you orphans. Christ by the gift of the Holy Spirit makes us one family in God our Father. We are members of a very large family, some two thousand years old. We need to get to know our relatives. The family history did not begin with Schleiermacher, nor indeed with the Reformers of the sixteenth century, nor even with St Thomas Aquinas and the builders of the great cathedrals. It is larger, more various and more exciting than that. It is indeed rooted in a history which goes back long before the time of Jesus and the apostles. The memory of Israel, of the events of Egypt and Sinai, of Jerusalem and the exile in Babylon, is constantly rendered present in the life and thought of all the Churches by their regular use of the Old Testament scriptures in their worship. The deserts of the Near East, the fertile hills and valleys of Palestine, the land flowing with milk and honey, these are images which have entered deeply into the heart of the whole Christian world. One of the most striking characteristics of the early Christian writings is the way in which the great figures of the history of Israel, Abraham and Moses, David and Elijah seem to be alive within the memory of the Church. If in subsequent centuries that memory has become dim for us, here is one of the causes of disunity and disintegration. This is why the meeting with Judaism as a living religion, the encounter with those who stand in direct succession to the prophets and the patriarchs is so very important for us.

When we come to the Christian centuries, it will already have become evident that for the point of view which this book expresses, the witness of Eastern Christendom is of vital significance, that half of the Christian world which is still below the horizon as far as most Western Christians are concerned. For every hundred books written about St Augustine, perhaps there is one written about St Maximus the Confessor. For every fifty books written about St John of the Cross, perhaps there is one on St Symeon the New Theologian. But these are figures of comparable stature. For a variety of reasons our Western faculties of theology have tended to ignore the whole development of Eastern Christian thought after the year 451. This is one of the reasons why the earlier period is so often misunderstood. But beyond that there is another Christian world lying on the farther side of the Byzantine Empire. There are the so-called 'lesser Eastern Churches', Coptic, Syrian, Armenian, Ethiopian, which remind us that Christianity is not, and has never been, a purely European-North American phenomenon. These Churches have immense and almost wholly unknown treasures. In the case of the Syrian tradition they link us back to the Semitic origins of our faith, revealing how the world of the New Testament grew in a Semitic environment, giving us great writers like St Ephrem and St Isaac the Syrian.

But it is not only to the East that we must turn. Nearer home there are treasures unknown to most of us. The more popular manifestations of Christian faith and devotion, the hymns, the prayers, the blessings, how little these are known, even when in the case of those of the Western Highlands they have an extraordinary beauty and depth. Then the minority movements are too often ignored. I think in particular of the Quakers with their unrivalled experience and understanding of the action of the Holy Spirit in creating unanimity amongst a group of free and often very different people, and the remarkable balance which they manage to preserve between real inwardness of spirit and social concern and action. Then there is the whole history of Christian liturgy, which touches in so many ways the worlds of music, architecture, poetry and painting. Surely the study of theology should include some introduction to the work of the supreme masters in these fields, to Andrei Rublev, to Dante, to Johann Sebastian Bach, to mention but three who happen to come from the three major divisions of Christendom.

And all this need not be eclectic or dilettante. For behind the differences of culture and tradition which mark these men, there are extraordinary if unperceived unities of faith and experience. All have prayed the Lord's Prayer, all have sought to follow the twin commandment of love of God and love of neighbour, all have confessed their faith in Father, Son and Holy Spirit. And if, by way of example, we take those three men, Bach, Rublev and Dante, and it is difficult to think of three human beings more different from one another, all will have prepared themselves for death by taking that food which Christians call the food of immortality.

Of course all this will be received by different people in very different ways, and with very different degrees of consciousness. But one of the greatest gifts of the Spirit to the Christian people is that of breaking down the barriers between popular culture and high culture, so that apparently very simple people may penetrate deeply into texts and prayers and symbols which our world would think esoteric, while very complicated people are enabled to find in the very plainness of the Gospel narratives a simplicity and a depth which the outsider can scarcely suspect. All this is at the very heart of the ecumenical movement, which is not primarily a matter of theological discussion, still less of ecclesiastical diplomacy, necessary though these things may be, but of a sense of a great and overarching order, of which we ourselves are part, a 'simultaneous order', which is called the communion of saints.

This movement of renewal helps us to rediscover ourselves and our own familiar tradition through our meeting with others. It makes us aware that the resources within the tradition to which we belong are much greater than we think. It gives us a glimpse of what the New Testament speaks about when it tells us of the new creation in Christ, not as an idea or a concept, but as a lived and living reality, revealing something of what the intersection of the timeless with time can mean for the time-bound, limited individual. There are unmeasured possibilities of love and knowledge, of joy and compassion, capacities of constructive action and creative work, which lie hidden in the heart and mind of man, and which are liberated when that heart and mind are opened to God and touched by the action of his grace. We sometimes see that this is so, in the face of a Mother Teresa of Calcutta, or of a John XXIII.

The awareness of this potential greatness of man, which is so utterly different from all the forms of secular 'greatness' which our age presents to us, speaks powerfully to our contemporaries. A young monk on Mount Athos, one of the many young men who in the last ten years have found in that ancient place a healing, liberating discipleship, wrote recently:

I am reading St Isaac the Syrian. I feel for the first time that there is a voice which resonates in the very depth of my being. Although he is so far removed in space and time, he has come right into my room, spoken to me, sat down beside me. For the first time I feel a kind of pride in our human nature; an amazement before it. He belongs to our common humanity. I rejoice at this. Being of the same nature as myself, he can transfuse the life-giving blood of this freedom into me. He reveals to me man in his true nature.[4]

In the 1960's a student in New York gave to me the following passage from another Isaac, Isaac of Stella, one of the first generation of Cistercians, which consists of an allegorical interpretation of the name of the original Isaac, the Son of Abraham, whose name means 'laughter'. 'Scripture says of the son of Abraham whose name signifies laughter, that he became very great (Gen. 26:13). My brother, may the Son of God who is already formed in you, grow in you so that for you he will become immeasurable, and that in you he will become laughter, exultation, the fulness of joy which no one will take from you.' [5] This is the immense and unbounded joy of the saints, which if it were not joined with a sense of man's weakness and fragility, would be nothing but madness. 'And if', Isaac goes on, 'you have sometimes forgotten this, or by negligence lost it, begin by the memory of him, to find his presence again'. This memory of God, lies at the heart and centre of all these other forms of remembering that we have been considering. It is when he remembers God that man finds himself again and finds that he is himself remembered.

II

But as we remarked at the beginning of this chapter, this Christian heritage of which we have been speaking, itself so vast and so diversified, needs to be seen in relation to other traditions, which themselves have inspired the devotion of generations of men and women. If, for example, we took this theme of 'the memory of

God' we should find it had a central place in many different ways of prayer and meditation.

How is the Christian tradition to be related to these other ways, Buddhist, Hindu, Jewish, Muslim? That is not a question to which we yet have an adequately formulated answer. Not, I am sure, by the dilution of what is specific in each tradition in an attempt to make it fit in with the others; that is to say, not in the case of Christianity by a reduction of the Christ to the stature of a great and inspired teacher who may be simply set alongside other such teachers. Nor by an attempt at a purely intellectual syncretism seeking to make some refined and metaphysical system in which all the differences will ultimately join. How these relationships are to be understood is not yet, I believe, clear. But that something is actually happening, that the traditions are actually meeting and interacting, and sometimes in a very profound and creative way, becomes more and more evident. There is already a great deal of responsible and highly qualified writing which bears witness to this meeting. It carries great and vital hopes for the future.

As regards Judaism and Islam, it is clear from the Christian point of view, that there is an immense amount of shared history and experience. All are children of Abraham, and walk by the faith of our father Abraham. Despite the obvious differences, they share large areas of common faith.

The history of our own century, with the appalling reality of the holocaust in the centre of Christian Europe and the subsequent establishment of the state of Israel, an event full of significance if also full of questions from a Christian or Jewish point of view, underlines the crucial importance of the development of Jewish-Christian dialogue. How can we begin to understand what God is saying in the events of this century, unless we are willing to listen to one another, and together to listen to him? Much more recently the enhanced economic and political importance of the Islamic nations, together with the signs of the resurgence of Islamic religion, has begun to make us more aware of the questions which the existence of this third great monotheism poses to us. The difficulties of dialogue ought not to blind us to its necessity.

One way in which the dialogue may begin, and is in fact already beginning, is in the areas of prayer and spirituality, for here the correspondences and comparisons between the traditions are numberless and fascinating. Through the writings of Martin Buber and others, the influence of Hasidism, the last great flowering of Jewish mysticism in the eighteenth and nineteenth centuries, on Christianity has already been considerable. It will almost certainly become stronger. As to the Sufi tradition in Islam, its attraction, even if sometimes at a superficial level, for many of our contemporaries is evident. The links which bind together Muslim and Christian devotion, especially in the early centuries of Islam are many, but they demand much further study and understanding. As the great and prophetic French scholar, Louis Massignon saw, there are signs of an interdependence here which most believers scarcely suspect.

But rather than examine these cognate areas in Judaism and Islam, I propose to turn to Hinduism, which is certainly further from us, in terms of geography and history, no less than of faith and teaching. And to contain the subject within reasonable limits I intend to look at our subject in the light of a book of outstanding quality, both as a work of scientific scholarship and imaginative interpretation, Raimundo Panikkar's *The Vedic Experience*. It is a book which sets out for us the Vedas, that collection of religious literature, covering at least fifteen hundred years, which contains hymns, prayers, and charms, as well as more reflective and philosophical treatises.

The Vedic Experience, a work of some nine hundred and fifty pages, has as it subtitle, *Mantramanjari, An Anthology of the Vedas for Modern Man and Contemporary Celebration*. This subtitle itself suggests something of the all-inclusive nature of the work. It is a collection of the classical texts of Hinduism, translated and annotated with the greatest care. But it is a collection made with a sense of urgency, with a contemporary need in mind, and so it also contains a considerable quantity of introductory material and commentary. The words with which the author addresses us at the beginning of his preface are these:

What would you save from a blazing house? A precious, irreplaceable manuscript containing a message of salvation for mankind, or a little group of people menaced by the same fire? The situation is real and not for this writer alone. How can you be just an 'intellectual' concerned with truth, or just a 'spiritual' busy with goodness, when men desperately cry for food and justice? How can you follow a contemplative, philosophical and religious path when the world shouts for action, engagement and politics? And conversely, how can you agitate for a better world or for the necessary revolution when what is most needed is serene insight and right evaluation?[6]

The author explains how for him the book has represented at least a partial resolution of the dilemma:

If I am not ready to save the manuscript from the fire, that is, if I do not take my intellectual vocation seriously, putting it before everything else even at the risk of appearing inhuman, then I am also incapable of helping people in more concrete and proximate ways. . . . If I do not involve myself in the concrete issues of my time, and if I do not open my house to all the winds of the world, then anything I may produce from an ivory tower will be barren and cursed. Yet if I do not shut doors and windows to concentrate on this work, then I will not be able to offer anything of value to my neighbours.[7]

This dilemma is one which has also been lying behind the preparation of these pages; certainly a very slender work by comparison with Panikkar's massive study, but even so, a work in which I have constantly been asking myself, 'am I advocating a mere antiquarianism, an escape into an earlier and supposedly golden age?'

The answer to these questions, I will give in the words of Raimundo Panikkar:

It is wise to remember that human memory and experience do not need to be reduced to those of the individual. One's real age is not necessarily to be reckoned by the number of times one's eyes have seen the sun encircle the earth. The Vedic experience may perhaps refresh a man's memory of his life on earth; it may be a reminder that he himself as well as his ancestors (though not only in and through them) has accumulated the most extraordinary experiences and has reached a depth of vision, feeling and life which he now urgently needs to rediscover if he is to succeed in breasting the waves of the ocean of technology, science and other modern devices, which threaten his very survival. The Vedic experience may perhaps disclose, not an alternative to the modern view of life and of the world, which would probably solve no problem and would certainly prove alienating, but an already existing, although often hidden, dimension of Man himself. It does not give 'information' about notions of the past, but truly 'in-forms' the present by allowing that dimension to appear and actually revealing it as a constituent part of Man's personhood. It is not only my individual past that is present in me; the history of Man too has accumulated in the cave of my heart, to use an Upanishadic expression; or, to put the same thought in another way, it is in the dendrites of my nervous system and in the DNA molecules. All these things are far older than my actual chronological age.[8]

Here is another view of the danger of temporal parochialism which besets our age, a view in some ways different from Eliot's, yet in many ways complementary to it. In both we see the distrust of a system of education which seems to provide information without conveying knowledge, which conveys knowledge without enabling any real growth in wisdom. In both we see the possibility of contemporary man coming to know himself to be part of a larger, more inclusive whole, and in both there is a sense of urgency about the need for this growth in vision.

In Hinduism no less than in Christianity it is vitally important that the words of the scriptures should become living words for us, should, as it were, come off the page and become our own words: 'When a word ceases to be a living word, when it ceases to convey meaning, when it is not a word for me, it is not a Veda, it does not convey real or saving knowledge.'[9] It is a statement which would have interesting implications if transferred to our methods of studying our Christian scriptures and celebrating our Christian liturgies. Of course the word 'celebration', which is used in the sub-title should not be too narrowly interpreted. Certainly it implies our active involvement. 'We have been saying' he remarks, 'that the reader is urged to study the texts, in the classical sense of the word "study", which includes not only intellectual effort but also voluntary commitment and human enthusiasm.'[10] But the enthusiasm, which is part of the study, may take different forms:

Celebration does not always mean jumping for joy nor is it always a festival of song and dance. It may include more inward and sober elements. It does, however, invariably contain the awareness that my acts have a deeper, more transcendent meaning than that which meets the eye, even though I myself may not be able to put this meaning into words. Celebration conveys a sense of cosmic solidarity, of human fellowship, and often of a divine accompaniment, by reason of which all our actions are liturgical, meaningful, expressive, both expressing what now is and creating what is about to be. There is no celebration without recurrence. What happens again and again is the proper subject of celebration as the word *celeber* suggests. We do not need to subscribe to a cyclical or spiral conception of time, but we do need a certain rhythmic consciousness in order truly to celebrate, that is, to transcend the petty routine of daily life which is so easily reduced, if there is no spirit of celebration, to a dispirited and humdrum mediocrity.[11]

Here again, it is implied, if we are to assimilate, we need to be assimilated. Only by participation are some things understood.

Panikkar is a Christian, a Roman Catholic priest. But he would not hesitate to describe himself as also a Hindu. In this book he insists that he is trying simply to expound the Vedas, in their own terms, or better to let the Vedas speak for themselves. He has purposely abstained from making comparisons or drawing out parallels. What he writes about prayer is for this reason, all the more impressive:

We use the traditional name of prayer, because from time immemorial when Man was led to pray, there was in the depths of his being, besides immediate motives such as fear, doubt, joy and gratitude, a still more powerful desire to hold his own life together and to hold it so together with the existence of the entire universe. Prayer can take many forms and we may pray for many immediate reasons, yet the common underlying assumption or implicit belief – though it may be worded variously according to different world views – is that in the act of prayer Man is sharing in the central dynamic of reality and penetrating into the heart of the world.[12]

In Christian terms we may say, as prayer links us to God so it also links us to the whole creation.

There are further implications to the act of prayer which bring us even closer to the themes of this book:

When he is at prayer, Man is not performing a private, individual act. He is performing a priestly action in the name of the whole of reality; he is the mediator between all possible extremes, the conductor line between all existing and conceivable tensions . . . Samdhyā is the prayer of time, for the world could not subsist if it were only a series of temporal successions. How could it pass from one instant to the next if there was no link between the two? The link is the Spirit, the spirit of prayer that unfolds in the mind and heart of the enlightened person, of the one who is rejuvenated by the waters and reborn by the rites of a second birth.[13]

The effect of such writing as this, is to make one anxious to refrain from easy and conventional comparisons between one religion and another. As we come to know something of another tradition, we become aware of meeting a whole new world of thought and reflection, of longing and aspiration, we come to realize a little more of the depth and extent of the human enterprise in which we are all in one way or other, engaged. It is of course true, that the Indian view of history and time is very different from that which would be shared by Christianity, Judaism and Islam, and that in general the Indian religions have given far less weight to time and history than has the Judaeo-Christian tradition. A serious study of the material will not lead us to underestimate the differences between them. Yet even at this point there are remarkable parallels with the lines of thought these pages have been seeking to explore. There is a sense that unless the moments of time are more than a mere linear succession of atoms, unless there is some overarching reality which links one to the other, then the world simply could not subsist. And in the realization of this link, the work and gift of prayer have an essential role to play.

But rather than speak about the Vedas, we must let the Vedas speak for themselves. Here are the last four verses of the Isa Upanishad, one of the most remarkable prayers in the whole tradition, and certainly one which bears directly upon our major theme. It is a prayer at sunrise, a prayer also connected with the time of death:

The face of Truth is covered over
by a golden vessel. Uncover it, O Lord,
that I who love the truth may see.
O Lord, sole Seer, Controller, Sun,
sun of the Father of beings, shine forth.
Concentrate your splendour that I may behold
your most glorious form. He who is yonder –
the Man yonder – I myself am he!
Go, my breath, to the immortal breath.
Then may this body end in ashes.
Remember, O my mind, the deeds of the past
remember the deeds, remember the deeds.
O Lord, lead us along the right path
to prosperity. O God, you know all our deeds.
Take from us our deceitful sin.
To you, then, shall we offer our prayers.[14]

Chapter 6

The Descent into Hell

Running throughout this book there have been references to the work of T. S. Eliot, in particular to two of his critical essays and to some of the outstanding passages of *Four Quartets*. In this chapter we shall listen once more to Eliot's words, in the first part looking in more detail at what he has to say to us in these four poems which are the culminating achievement of his poetic genius. In the second part we shall seek to confront the questions which he raises in the light of the Scriptures of the Christian tradition.

From the opening lines of *Burnt Norton* to the concluding section of *Little Gidding*, the theme of time present and time past, their relationship and meaning, is never far from the surface in the *Four Quartets*. As we have already seen, *Burnt Norton* begins with the words

> Time present and time past
> Are both perhaps present in time future . . . (I, 1–2)[1]

It is a tentative statement, a statement which captures the mood of this whole poem, elusive, shining, hinting at meanings not yet articulated. But some things are already clear. Life when it is entirely confined to the dimensions of past and present, to a totally linear view of time becomes futility, 'a twittering world'. And this is very much the condition of our civilization, as we hear in *The Dry Salvages*.

> When there is distress of nations and perplexity
> Whether on the shores of Asia, or in the Edgware Road.

Men's curiosity searches past and future
And clings to that dimension . . . (V, 197–200)

This condition is linked inescapably with the failure of our society to confront the fact of death, the moment when for the individual time comes to an end. Our inability to prepare for death, our failure to realize the importance of this moment in the life of man, our unwillingness even to look at the body after death, an object of a sometimes startling beauty, are all signs and symptoms of a disquieting failure on the part of our civilization. Earlier societies, whatever their own weaknesses and limitations may have been, had their rituals for meeting this moment of crisis. We seem helpless before it. The threat of death and meaninglessness, so powerfully felt in Eliot's earlier poetry, is still strongly present in the work of his maturity. It is part of its greatness that it confronts the matter so directly. How is death to be overcome? Where is meaning to be found? Meaning is found, or better, given at moments which seem to be outside time, and which we may at first be tempted to think are without relation to time. But, in fact, it is at such moments, 'At the still point of the turning world', that we find that 'past and future are gathered'. And in the course of time as the timeless moments are recalled, we find that it is 'only through time that time is conquered'. Time and eternity are more closely inter-related than we thought. They can lead us into a movement towards meaning which is contrasted in the last lines of the poem with the futility of a time unredeemed by such moments of insight:

Ridiculous the waste sad time
Stretching before and after. (V, 174–5)

East Coker is by contrast a poem full of the images of earth and of the turning seasons. It seems to represent a kind of personal reconciliation with the rhythms of nature, and with the rise and fall of families and houses. East Coker was after all the home of Eliot's ancestors, the place where he chose to be buried, and the poem contains a quotation from the work of his sixteenth century forebear, Sir Thomas Elyot. So now the timeless moment is seen as more closely intertwined with the patterns of the seasons and with the patterns of history, personal and national:

As we grow older

109

The world becomes stranger, the pattern more complicated
Of dead and living. Not the intense moment
Isolated, with no before and after,
But a life-time burning in every moment
And not the life-time of one man only
But of old stones that cannot be deciphered. (V, 190–196)

The awareness of the growing strangeness of the patterns of time
and life as we ourselves grow older recurs in the following poem:

It seems, as one becomes older
That the past has another pattern, and ceases to be a mere
sequence –
Or even development . . . (II, 85–88)

The fleeting moments of ecstasy contained within themselves
meanings of which we were not aware at the time:

And approach to the meaning restores the experience
In a different form, beyond any meaning
We can assign to happiness. I have said before
That the past experience revived in the meaning
Is not the experience of one life only
But of many generations – not forgetting
Something that is probably quite ineffable: (II, 94–100)

Here surely are lines which betray a long and reflective experience of liturgical worship, in which the past experience is constantly
'revived in the meaning', and in which the experience of many
generations becomes accessible to us, in a moment at which that
which is beyond all speech, the very mystery of God, draws near.

But in *The Dry Salvages* something happens which alters the
tone of the discussion. In this poem Eliot speaks of the Incarnation
with a directness which he generally avoids in these poems. It is
striking, for instance, that neither the Father, the Son, nor the
Holy Spirit are ever named by those names in *The Four Quartets*.
Everywhere present they are never addressed. This is a fact which
in any full theological investigation of these poems would need to
be discussed at length. Does it tell us something about the necessary
indirectness of all poetic affirmation of the divine, or does it speak

of the particular problems and difficulties of such statement in our own time? But here at least, there is an explicit reference to the:

hardly, barely prayable
Prayer of the one Annunciation. (II, 83–4)

And Section IV appropriately consists of a prayer to our Lady, or to be more accurate a request for her prayers, and contains a quotation from Dante.

Figlia del tuo figlio
Queen of heaven. (IV, 177–8)

Something unusually important is happening here, which bears directly on our major concerns. As Harry Blamires remarks in his commentary *Word Unheard*, 'The emphatic definition of the Virgin's paradoxical role, as the most human daughter of the divine Son and the Queen of Heaven, itself sharply elucidates the end and destination to which the poem's explanatory hints and guesses, sudden illuminations and discursive speculations, are all alike leading, and foreshadows the coming utterance of the word "Incarnation" in the next movemt. Moreover the use of Dante's phrase, "Figlia del tuo figlio", by its directness and explicitness, injects into the poem a concentrated infusion of allusive overtones of a kind which oblique and less readily identifiable literary echoes establish only gradually. . . . What is hinted at in man's intermittent glimpses of the eternal, the sudden shafts of sunlight momentarily transfiguring the world, is rendered fully articulate in the incarnation of God in man.'[2]

We are not therefore surprised in the final section of this poem to find the explicit formulation 'the point of intersection of the timeless and time', as Eliot's way of stating the meaning of the Incarnation:

But to apprehend
The point of intersection of the timeless
With time, is an occupation for the saint –
No occupation either, but something given
And taken, in a lifetime's death in love,
Ardour and selflessness and self-surrender.
For most of us, there is only the unattended

111

Moment, the moment in and out of time,
The distraction fit, lost in a shaft of sunlight. . . .
These are only hints and guesses
Hints followed by guesses; and the rest
Is prayer, observance, discipline, thought and action.
The hint half-guessed, the gift half understood, is Incarnation.
Here the impossible union
Of spheres of action is actual,
Here the past and future
Are conquered and reconciled. . . . (V, 200 ff)

There is much here that calls for comment. To see incarnation as something which is constantly taking place is a thought more deeply rooted in Christian tradition than perhaps even Eliot realized. Maximus the Confessor, for instance, sees God becoming incarnate in all things, especially in the lives of his servants. He becomes man, in them, so that in him they may become God. 'The Word of God, who is God, wills always and in all things to work the mystery of his Incarnation.' Eliot's theological intuition here as elsewhere is outstanding. Yet at the very same moment, the complete division between the saint and the ordinary believer – which one finds again in *The Cocktail Party* – is, in this form, not wholly true either to tradition or experience. Doubtless there are an indefinite number of degrees of Christian commitment possible, but apart from the fact that the New Testament clearly thinks that all believers are called to be saints, even the saints have their moments of distraction – as Thomas Merton remarks, the hermit finds he has an ulcer like the next man and has to drink quantities of milk – while the ordinary believer, under his apparent ordinariness may often conceal something like heroic virtue. To have maintained his own strict adherence to the Church's faith and practice, in the circles in which Eliot moved must at times have required something like heroic constancy.

But what is primary in this passage is that here the moment where heaven and earth meet, where God and man are united, is recognized as the place where past and future are not abolished or denied, but reconciled and brought together. It is also the moment of death, but of 'death in love', that is to say, death into life.

It is this thought which is developed much further in *Little*

Gidding. In this poem it is the image of fire which predominates. It is the poem of the Spirit, of death, and of prayer. It is also the poem of pilgrimage. All the *Quartets* are rooted in one clearly defined, closely observed place, but here the place is a place of pilgrimage, because quite explicitly a place of incarnation.

> If you came this way,
> Taking any route, starting from anywhere,
> At any time or at any season,
> It would always be the same: you would have to put off
> Sense and notion. You are not here to verify,
> Instruct yourself, or inform curiosity
> Or carry report. You are here to kneel
> Where prayer has been valid. And prayer is more
> Than an order of words, the conscious occupation
> Of the praying mind, or the sound of the voice praying.
> And what the dead had no speech for, when living
> They can tell you, being dead: the communication
> Of the dead is tongued with fire beyond the language of the
> living.
> Here, the intersection of the timeless moment
> Is England and nowhere. Never and always. (I, 39 ff)

Many of the themes which we have touched on in these pages here find unrivalled expression. In prayer, the mystery of the relation of past and present is illumined through the action of the Holy Spirit, who moves and burns in the depths of man's spirit. In prayer the mind is carried up through words beyond words, through time beyond time into a silence which is full of meaning and full of presence, full indeed of time, because it is the silence of an eternity, which is not the negation but the fulfilment of time. And so in the moment of prayer the past can be present in a way which conveys more not less reality, more not less meaning than it did in the moment when it was itself 'present'. It is a past which is full of the riches of eternity.

But there is another point here which demands attention. In this poem Eliot uses the word 'England' three times, (it occurs nowhere else in the *Quartets*) and always with considerable emphasis. We are told that this place, Little Gidding, is the nearest "now and in

113

England", and later at a moment of climax in the poem, we are told again

> So, while the light fails
> On a winter's afternoon, in a secluded chapel
> History is now and England. (V, 235–7)

There were doubtless pressing reasons to be more than usually aware of the national tradition in 1942. It stood menaced as seldom before. But even so this triple invocation of the name of England, has something particularly moving about it, and reminds us how great was Eliot's love for the land of his ancestry and his adoption. It may, for instance, help those who are English by birth to renew their own love for their country, and to find for it a love which is neither sentimental, arrogant nor exclusive. It is a sad and disturbing fact of our times, that when love of country is spoken of, and it very seldom is, it should so often be done in terms which are sentimental and uncritical, arrogant and exclusive. That is the way of a blind and destructive nationalism, which has little in common with a love for one's own country which helps one to love all other countries, and which recognizes that all nations have their part in the universal design of God. Very different is the insight which recognizes that it is only in particular times and places, only in that wedding of time and place which makes the history of a people or an individual, that incarnation can be fully realised.

One of the things which makes the particular strength of this poem is precisely this, that its most universal statements are made in such specific ways. Section II which involves a kind of descent into hell evokes not only Dante and the *Purgatorio*, but the London of the air-raids, the nightly fire-watching patrols with their constant possibility of death. It reminds us very directly and very simply of man's approach to his end, of the need to be honest in face of the bitterness and diminution of old age and death. Only so can the Spirit carry through a work which must be first pain and purification before it can be delight. Only through death is the pattern of the temporal and eternal revealed. And it is in the statements of the section which follows (Section III) that Eliot is able to expound with an astonishing clarity so many of the points which he has been gradually exploring:

114

This is the use of memory:
For liberation – not less of love but expanding
Of love beyond desire, and so liberation
From the future as well as the past. Thus, love of a country
Begins as attachment to our own field of action
And comes to find that action of little importance
Though never indifferent. History may be servitude,
History may be freedom. See, now they vanish,
The faces and places, with the self, which, as it could, loved
them,
To become renewed, transfigured in another pattern.
Sin is behovely, but
All shall be well, and
All manner of thing shall be well. (III, 156–168)

The moment of incarnation, fully present in history, yet opening
history to what is beyond it, frees us from the servitudes of history.
History is fulfilled, the history of a people, no less than of an
individual, when it transcends itself into the kingdom of eternity.
The true use of memory is that through the things which are called
to mind we should be liberated into the kingdom of God, by an
experience of love beyond desire; in which because we can remember with thanksgiving we can give back to God what rightly belongs
to him. This involves a renunciation of those obsessions which can
imprison nations no less than individuals in the memory of past
griefs and injustices. There is surely here a reminiscence of the
teaching of St John of the Cross, which links memory with hope.
As we give up the clinging to the past, so the memory of the past
becomes part of our way towards God, who is also Lord of the
future.

There follow in the poem the lines which recall briefly, but with
great vividness, the figures who were locked in combat in the Civil
War, the King himself, Milton, the regicides, the family at Little
Gidding, and implicit within them the tension between Old and
New England which played so large a part in Eliot's own devel-
opment. We are not now to revive these ancient controversies. In
death their protagonists have been united in the infinite mercy of
God:

And all shall be well and

All manner of thing shall be well
By the purification of the motive
In the ground of our beseeching. (III, 196–9)

So in the last section of the poem, there comes a final statement
about time and history, a statement which again is as true for each
one as it is for a whole people, as true for the poet himself as for
the country which he had chosen:

A people without history
Is not redeemed from time, for history is a pattern
Of timeless moments. So, while the light fails
On a winter's afternoon, in a secluded chapel
History is now and England. (V, 234–8)

II

After the splendour of Eliot's lines it seems almost perverse to try
to say the same things again in a different idiom. But perhaps the
very contrast may help to bring out the underlying convergences
of meaning. At least after the subtlety of poetry, here is a little of
the bluntness of theological prose, an attempt to refer directly to
that moment of intersection of the timeless with time which is the
heart of Christian faith and worship.

At the beginning of this book we remarked on the fact that it is
the inescapable reference to the person of Jesus Christ himself,
which necessarily involves Christians in a reference to the past.
Perhaps after considering a poem which is full of the presence of
the Holy Spirit we can begin to see why it is that when reference
is made to Christ *alone*, it is likely to lead us into insoluble difficulties. For Jesus Christ as we see him in the Gospels is never
alone. His life is lived in constant relationship to the Father. He is
the one who is filled with the Spirit and himself bestows the Spirit
on his disciples. We see him always in relationship, never in isolation. The picture of Jesus in the Gospels is inescapably Trinitarian. And the pattern of divine relationships which is focussed in
him, is mirrored in the pattern of human relationships which grows

116

up around him. He binds his disciples together into one; they become one, as he and the Father are one. When we begin to see our subject in terms of these relationships we begin to see our way through some of the difficulties.

Let us briefly consider two moments of crucial importance in the ministry of Jesus, both of which in the Gospel narratives involve a revelation of the presence of the Father and the Spirit, i.e. the Baptism and the Transfiguration. In the first instance, Jesus goes down into the water of Jordan, the Father's voice is heard declaring 'This is my beloved Son in whom I am well pleased', the Spirit is seen descending as a dove. Jesus is the anointed one, the Messiah; the one who is Christ. In the Orthodox tradition it is this incident which is commemorated on the Feast of Epiphany, commemorated precisely as a revelation of God's nature as Trinity. But the moment of the baptism does not only contain this vertical, transcendent reference. It is not only a point of intersection of the timeless with time. It is also a point in which there is a gathering together of time into a moment of fulness. There is a horizontal dimension which is also vital, a recalling of the past, a turning to the future. The act of receiving baptism clearly marks Jesus' identification with the whole history of the people to whom he belongs, he makes himself one with them in their need for repentance, one with them in this proclamation of faith. It may also have a more universal significance. Going down into the waters may signify going down into the unconscious, into the primal chaos on which God's Spirit moves in order to bring order. It certainly prefigures Jesus going down into death. The Byzantine texts for this feast speak of Jesus as going down into the water 'to raise up a fallen world'. The whole past is recapitulated. The future is no less clearly anticipated. This is the moment at which Jesus, filled with the Spirit, goes out into the desert to do battle with the devil, before beginning his ministry of healing, teaching and proclaiming the Kingdom, the ministry which is to lead him to the Cross.

What is seen at the baptism, is seen even more clearly at the moment of the Transfiguration. Here Jesus has taken the three chosen disciples, Peter and James and John, into a high mountain apart. He is transfigured before them. Moses and Elijah appear with him. A bright cloud descends upon them, a cloud signifying the presence of the divine glory, the coming of the Holy Spirit.

117

Once again the voice is heard, 'This is my beloved Son: hear him'. The Trinitarian nature of the experience is again clearly evident. The disciples see Jesus as he really is, in his unique relationship to the Father, the one on whom the Spirit rests in all his fulness. But the threefold reference in time becomes even more explicit. Human figures are associated with Jesus in his glory, figures from the past, no less than disciples in the present, those to whom the future will belong. In the persons of Moses and Elijah, the representative figures of the Law and the Prophets, the whole history of the Old Testament is resumed. In the persons of Peter, James and John, the whole Church is present in embryo. In them we too are participants in the mystery.

Again we can surely see a more universal reference here, which in no way dilutes the particular historical one. Jesus goes up into a mountain to pray, as men have done since the earliest times of human history. This holy mountain is as it were the focal point, the gathering place of so many holy mountains. But the reference forward has a particular point to it. In St Luke's account we read that Jesus is speaking with Moses and Elijah, about the exodus which he is to accomplish in Jerusalem. His death is explicitly foreshadowed, and beyond it his glorification. And all this takes place in a moment of intense and heightened consciousness. If the baptism is a moment of epiphany, of the manifestation of God's glory, how much more is this moment. It is the very heart of all such moments, made known in an indefinite number of ways, known for instance with a particular vividness to those who are given some form of artistic vision, known in another way, less clear but perhaps more universal and profound, at moments when we realize the inescapable nature of the choice between good and evil, known above all with a particular fulness in the worship of the Church when in the presence of God, future and past are drawn together into one, and the pattern or shape of human life and destiny is for a moment disclosed.

But these two moments are themselves on the way to that supreme moment, in which as St John's Gospel says, God's glory is to be revealed, the moment of supreme irony and paradox, when as it seems everything falls apart and Christ dies upon the cross. Is there a different pattern revealed here? Is our exposition of the moments of baptism and transfiguration perhaps too neat and tidy?

Will it prove adequate to this supreme moment of reversal? And in this age in which we live, the age of the critical intellect, and of the advance of the absurd, what sense can we make of stories of transfiguration and resurrection?

Let us begin from this moment at which we live. It is the moment which we are given, we have no other. If we are to come into contact with eternity it must be here and now. There is no other possibility. It is certain that the fact of death weighs on our age with a particular heaviness. Our very anxiety not to speak of it, hints at its all-pervasive presence. Belsen, Hiroshima, the Gulag Archipelago, the massacres in Cambodia, these haunt our minds consciously and unconsciously. And with this sense of death there comes a sense of meaninglessness. As Saunders Lewis has put it, 'the crisis which is weighing upon Christians and ex-Christians today is not a crisis of guilt, but of doubt as to whether life has any meaning at all. There is plenty of reason for this despair; there are two world wars, with the likelihood and near-certainty that there will be a third which will put an end to civilization and perhaps to the human race. Concentration camps like Belsen and Dauchau remain with us as symbols of the value we attach to human beings.' [3]

So it is that in our lives there often seems to be no meaning. The artists who are our contemporaries present us with frightening images of human disintegration – one thinks of the canvases of Francis Bacon. The carefully worked patterns of nineteenth century drama and fiction give way to the theatre of the absurd. Can there be any longer an intelligible outline to things? Eliot saw all this already more than half a century ago. And yet the poet of *The Waste Land* became the poet of *Ash Wednesday*, the poet of the *Four Quartets*, and it is not necessary to see that progression as a decline. Rather it could be seen as a development with a significance which is far more than individual. For the faith which Eliot embraced is a faith that even there, into the depths of hell, into the place where life and meaning are absent, Christ has gone, even there the light has been revealed, even there hope and meaning have triumphed over despair.

Here is a further point where the tradition of the Eastern Church has a particular and urgent relevance for our own day. For without question this thought of the descent into hell, this meditation on the meaning of Christ's death, has been far more fully developed and expressed in the rites of the Christian East than in the West. The services for Holy Week provide us with a rich material for theological reflection. 'Hell is king over mortal men, but not for ever. Laid in the sepulchre, mighty Lord, with thy life-giving hand thou hast burst asunder the bars of death. To those from every age who slept in the tombs, thou hast proclaimed true deliverance, O Saviour, who art become the first-born from the dead.' [4] It is a universal liberation which gathers together those from every age, since the beginning of mankind until the day of judgement. It is Adam and Eve who are pulled up from darkness. 'Thou hast united all that before was separated; wrapped in a winding-sheet, O Saviour, and buried in a tomb, thou hast loosed the prisoners, and they cry: "There is none holy save thee, O Lord." ' [5] But this act of deliverance, though it is universal is also intimately personal. There is nothing generalized about it. I am in Adam, Adam is in me. 'To fill all things with thy glory, thou hast gone down into the nethermost parts of the earth: for my person that is in Adam has not been hidden from thee, but in thy love for man thou art buried in the tomb and dost restore me from corruption.' [6] From my own personal hell of despondency and self-destruction, of paralysing guilt and anxiety, from a strait-jacket of circumstances not of my own devising, I myself am lifted up, restored to true relationship, by him who descended into death to find me. 'To earth hast thou come down, O Master, to save Adam: and not finding him on earth, thou hast descended into hell, seeking him there.' [7]

All this is the work not of some universal, impersonal principle. It is wrought out in the body of Jesus of Nazareth, in whom we see that:

One of the Trinity suffered in the flesh. . . . Every member of thy holy body endured dishonour for our sakes; thy head, the thorns; thy face, the spitting; thy cheeks, the buffeting; thy mouth, the taste of gall mingled with vinegar; thine ears, the impious blasphemies; thy back, the scourging and thy hand, the reed; thy whole body, the stretching on the cross; thy limbs, the nails; and thy side, the spear. Thou hast suffered for us and by thy passion set us free from passions; in loving self-abasement

120

thou hast stooped down to us and raised us up: O Saviour almighty have mercy on us.[8]

Jesus is identified with the tortured, the imprisoned, the victims of injustice and of every kind of inhumanity. He suffers in them. They are included in him. As he is pulled apart, so he draws all things together into one. This is no figure of speech; the body is manhandled as in a contemporary torture-chamber. 'Stretched out upon the wood, thou hast drawn mortal men into unity; pierced in thy life-giving side, O Jesu, thou art become a fountain of forgiveness unto all.' [9] The whole is summed up in the amazing words, 'The whole creation was altered by thy passion: for all things suffered with thee, knowing, O Word, that thou holdest all things in unity'.[10]

We see this very simply in the words which the Evangelists declare that Jesus uttered on the cross. The first three of his utterances are concerned with others, drawing together those who are around him, the men who are carrying out the execution, the robbers who are his companions in suffering, his mother and his friend who stand beside the cross. In the words which follow, it is his relationship with the Father which is affirmed, even in the greatest and most terrible of all, 'My God, my God, why hast thou forsaken me?'

All things were altered by Christ's passion, past and future, East and West. Time and space are no longer barriers which separate us from one another, but ways of communion, paths by which we may come to meet one another in the life which flows from the side of Christ. Injury itself, evil and wrong, all that can cause men and women to hate and destroy one another, that too is overcome, for with life there comes forgiveness, the life-giving power of reconciliation and peace. One thing which is very clear in the ancient rites for Holy Week both of East and West is that Christ's death can never be separated from his resurrection; the cross is life-giving. 'We venerate thy cross, O lord, and sing and tell the glory of thy holy resurrection, for by virtue of the cross, joy is come into the whole world.' [11] So it is that in the East the icon of the resurrection is the icon of the descent into hell, Christ's triumphant passage through the gates of death, drawing up with him Adam and Eve and all the race of man. This is what faith in Christ's resurrection

121

means. As Julian of Norwich puts it: 'At this point he began first to show his might, for then he went into hell; and when he was there, then he raised up the great root out of the deep darkness, which rightfully was knit to him in high heaven. The body lay in the grave till Easter morrow; and from that time he lay never more.' (cp. 51)[12]

If we return to the origins of Christian faith in the New Testament, and especially in the Gospel of St John, we find further that the resurrection is never to be separated from the coming of the Spirit. In the narrative of the Fourth Gospel, it is on the very day of his rising from the dead that Jesus imparts the Spirit to his disciples. And however the fifty days, which in the synoptic Gospels intervene between the resurrection and the outpouring of the Spirit, are to be interpreted, it is clear that the one event follows on directly from the other, that neither can be understood without the other. The event of Christ is completed in the coming of the Spirit. The event of Pentecost is in no way to be understood except in terms of all that has preceded it. Rather we may say that it is at Pentecost that that which was done secretly in the depths of the earth while Jesus lay buried in the tomb, is now proclaimed openly for all to see. All men are called into this new unity which God's forgiving love has created. The life which has been won through death, is now made known in him who is the Lord and Life-giver.

The Trinitarian pattern which we observed earlier is therefore to be found here too, though because the material is richer and more complex it is perhaps not so immediately discernible. Christ in the power of the Spirit, offers himself in love to the Father; and it is the Spirit of the Father who raises Jesus triumphant over death. And here even more clearly is a gathering together of past and future in *the* moment of the intersection of the timeless with time. The past is redeemed, changed by the present in ways we can neither understand nor imagine, but which fulfil a deep and incoherent longing in our nature. The future is opened up as a future which is ruled by faith, by hope, by love. Already the Kingdom of eternity begins to become present in time, time begins to be gathered up into the fulness of eternity. The tradition which is handed on through time, is itself at every moment dependent on that other and greater tradition, the handing over of the Spirit from eternity to time. The whole creation is held in being by the two hands of God, the Son and the Spirit – the terms are those of St Irenaeus – the two hands of love which fashion out of the chaos of our lives an order which reflects the beauty and the life which is in heaven.

But all this is to be realized now in the last years of the twentieth century and in the first years of the twenty-first, here in a world which is menaced in so many ways by destruction, absurdity and death. What hope can there be that the scattered Christian Churches can be so renewed in unity and life that they may become a credible witness to the reality of Christ's resurrection? At the beginning we referred to that central act of Christian worship, the one distinctive thing which almost all Christians do when they come together, the act which is performed 'in remembrance' of the one who instituted it. It is an interesting and, to a Christian, highly encouraging fact that in the last twenty years, a number of agreements have been reached about this sacrament between Churches which have long been at variance with one another about its meaning, and that in these agreements two elements are nearly always present.

First, it is agreed that the words just quoted are to be understood in a very strong and positive sense. In the Eucharist we do not remember a Master long-since dead and absent. We recall one who in the act of recalling becomes present with us. Here above all is the effective presence of the past in the present. Secondly, it is agreed that all this happens in the power and energy of the Holy Spirit. The belief that in the Eucharist the Spirit is active, that the Sacrament is in some sense the constant presence of Pentecost in the Church, as well as the constant presence of Christ's death and resurrection, has always had a central place in the theology of the Christian East. In the West amongst Catholics and many Protestants it has been not so much rejected as forgotten – John Calvin is an honourable exception here, and so are the Scottish divines who stand in succession to the doctors of Aberdeen. Suddenly within the last twenty years this element of belief has become powerful again amongst Catholics and Protestants alike. It has proved to be a help on the way to resolving old controversies and to discovering new meanings. It is expressed in every one of the new Eucharistic prayers in use throughout the Roman Catholic Church. As the Anglican-Roman Catholic International Commission expresses it, 'By the transforming action of the Spirit of God, earthly bread and wine become the heavenly manna and the new wine, the eschatological banquet for the new man; elements of the first creation become pledges and first-fruits of the new heaven and the new earth'.[13]

Here are modest signs of the growing power of the Spirit in the Church, signs that the kingdom which is to come is even now making itself known, and showing the way towards the future. These agreements in faith and doctrine are, of course, only one element within a whole fabric of movements of rediscovery and reconciliation in which, in many different ways and in many different places Christians are finding anew their unity in Christ and the Spirit. Some of these involve practical collaboration in helping the poor and disadvantaged and in struggling for justice and peace. Others bring Christians together in new experiences of prayer and worship. Others are concerned with a united witness to the truth of the Gospel. There are powers of new life and insight here which we ought not to underestimate.

What the future will hold it is not possible to say, but perhaps what we have seen from the past may suggest to us that it could convey a new realization of the unity of the human family, not only at the outward and social level, but also at the deepest point of experience where all men and women have to face the mysteries of suffering, tragedy and death, and seek to see beyond them. In Christ that unity is already in principle given to us. It also could convey a new sense of the kinship of all mankind, not only in the present, but across the generations, helping us to reverse the myth of Oedipus, and reminding us of the inner discoveries made by societies other than our own, which have concentrated more of their attention and their love on things within, rather than on the world around them. The life of the Spirit of God within man's spirit opens up unlimited possibilities of that love and knowledge for which man was created. It could convey the possibility of a new attitude to this world, an attitude of contemplative and appreciative delight, rather than one of a compulsive desire to exploit and manipulate. When we cease to cling to the things which are around us we find that all things are ours to rejoice in and enjoy. These are possibilities which can open up for us as we regain a sense of the way in which the lives of all of us are bound together, and how it is that all together we need to receive this life as a gift, a gift which is full of the goodness and truth which comes from the transcendent Giver, the Maker of all things.

Epilogue

'The World Is Charged With the Grandeur of God'

At the heart of Christian worship there is an affirmation and acknowledgement of the transcendent majesty and glory of God. 'Holy, holy, holy;' these are the characteristic words of Christian prayer and praise. But what is not always noticed is that this movement of adoration is inseparably linked with a proclamation of God's glory revealed in his creation. So in the vision of Isaiah, the seraphim cry, 'Holy, holy, holy is the Lord of hosts: the whole earth is full of his glory'.[1] Consider again the cry of the heavenly powers in the book of Revelation. 'Thou art worthy, O Lord our God, to receive glory and honour and power because thou didst create all things; by thy will they were created and have their being.'[2] God is worshipped as creator of all and all creation is associated in this worship. 'Then I heard every created thing in heaven and on earth and under the earth and in the sea, all that is in them, crying, "praise and honour, glory and might to him who sits on the throne and to the Lamb, for ever and ever." '[3]

If we turn to the Psalms, which, in varying forms and in different ways, have played so central a part in the whole history of Christian worship, we shall find exactly the same thing. All creation praises the Lord, angels and heavenly powers, beasts and birds, plants and living things, the earth itself, the seas, the stars, all enter with man into the worship of him whose glory is revealed in all that he has made. 'O Lord, how manifold are thy works; in wisdom hast thou made them all; the earth is full of thy riches.'[4]

The perception of God's transcendent holiness is in no sense at war with the perception of the presence and activity of his glory in all that he has made. And the praise of God in and through his whole creation is in no way at war with the recognition of the particular nature of his creation of man, or of his call to Israel his people. Time and again in the Psalms the universal hymn of all things is linked with the praise and thanksgiving of God's people for particular mercies and blessings. In the New Testament, all God's acts towards his people are summed up and fulfilled in the great redemption wrought in Jesus Christ, our Lord. To the praise of the Creator is joined the praise of the Redeemer. 'Worthy is the Lamb, the Lamb that was slain to receive all power and wealth, wisdom and might, honour and glory and praise.' [5] It is not one thing or another, either a God beyond or a God within, either a God in history or a God in nature. It is and it must be these three things together. So in the bush which burns but is not consumed, perhaps the most eloquent of all the symbols of God's glory seen throughout creation, the Name of God is revealed, revealed in its transcendent and universal majesty, 'I am that I am', revealed also in the particularity of God's faithfulness to his people, 'The Lord God of your fathers, the God of Abraham, the God of Isaac and the God of Jacob.' [6]

If we now take a text from the heart of the Christian tradition of worship we shall find the same pattern. Here is a prayer which is used Sunday by Sunday in all the parishes of the Eastern Ortho- dox Church, in Greek and Slavonic, in Arabic and Romanian, in Bulgarian and Finnish in French and English. Immediately after the choir have sung the hymn 'Holy, holy, holy,' the celebrant in the *Liturgy of St John Chrysostom* continues in these words:

And with these blessed powers, O Master and lover of man, we also cry and say, Holy and most holy art thou, thou and thine only-begotten Son and thy Holy Spirit; holy and most holy art thou in the majesty of thy glory, who hast so loved thy world that thou didst give thine only begotten Son, that all who believe in him should not perish but have eternal life, who being come and having accomplished all that was appointed for our sake, in the night in which he was given up, or rather gave up himself for the life of the world, took bread into his holy, pure and spotless hands, and having given thanks and blessed and hallowed it, he gave it to his disciples and apostles saying. . . .[7]

This text, which recent scholarship has tended to affirm to be the work of John Chrysostom himself, makes again the same point that we have seen in Isaiah, in the Psalms, in Revelation. The most emphatic and insistent affirmation of God's transcendent holiness, utterly beyond what man can think or desire, is linked at once with the confession that he who made all things, has made himself fully known in flesh and blood, has taken into his hands the bread and wine which are the strength of man's life on earth, has revealed himself fully in the dying and rising of Jesus the Lord. All those affirmations are made together, the transcendence of God's glory, the immanence of his activity, the revelation of his love in the incarnation of the Word.

II

I have begun with an appeal to Scripture and the praying tradition of the early centuries of the Church's history, long before the schism between East and West and the separations of the sixteenth century, in order to assert that these closely linked themes of the revelation of God's glory in and through the created universe, and the place of the material creation in the prayer and praise which we offer to God, are not peripheral or secondary to our concern for Christian worship. Rather, they are essential to the fulness of the tradition. The whole earth, not man alone, is the temple of God's glory. Man comes before God not in isolation from the rest of creation, not in mind and heart alone, but in the fulness of his being, bodily as well as spiritual, social as well as personal, bringing with him all this material universe of which he forms a part. As we shall see, our faith in Christ's incarnation, our faith in his bodily resurrection, and in the resurrection of our bodies, carries with it implications of a universal scope.

But the title of this chapter is taken not from Scripture or from the tradition of the early centuries. It comes from a poet of nineteenth-century England, Gerard Manley Hopkins:

The world is charged with the grandeur of God
It will flame out, like shining from shook foil. . . .[8]

Is the work of the poets of the last hundred years really able to
bear so much weight? Can we legitimately put their writings alongside the Scriptures of the Church, in the way in which we did in
the previous chapter? Is this not to claim altogether too much for
the inspiration of the poet?

Let us say at once that in a world which is everywhere marked
by the fall, man's poetic capacities in no way escape the general
ambiguities of our sinful situation. This gift no less than any other
can be abused. The devil can disguise himself as an angel of light.
But let us also remark that a large part of the language of the
Scriptures is poetic; much of the Prophets, much of the Book of
Revelation, not to speak of the whole of the Psalms, and the Book
of Job. And a large part of the language of Christian worship down
the ages is also the language of poetry; the whole vast heritage of
Christian hymnody, much larger than we usually realize, not to
speak of the wealth of poetic prose to be found in the various forms
of liturgical prayer. We shall not get very far in understanding the
language of the Psalms, or in penetrating into the meaning of
Christian prayer and praise, unless we are becoming sensitive to
the nature and value of poetic language. It is a language which, in
its own way, the way of images and not of concepts, is as precise
and exacting as the clearest and most carefully reasoned prose. It
is a language which binds many meanings together into unity rather
than attempting to isolate a single one, which gathers together and
does not divide, which speaks to man's heart as well as to his
intellect. At its best it can unify the different elements of man's
being, conscious and unconscious, discursive and intuitive, into a
single act of utterance and praise. For it is above all the language
of praise,[9] in which man, is carried out beyond himself towards
the one he praises, a language in which, in some degree, man
transcends the daily limitations of his lot.

While in the past we find that a large proportion of the texts
which have been used in Christian worship, particularly those
which speak of God's glory revealed in all creation, have been of
a highly poetic nature, in our own time neither this quality nor this
theme has been particularly evident in the public preaching and

teaching of our Churches. But it has found magnificent expression in the work of some of the many Christian poets God has given to our age. Let us, for example, take a passage from the work of one of the best-loved of recent Scottish poets, Edwin Muir:

> So from the ground we felt that virtue branch
> Through all our veins till we were whole, our wrists
> As fresh and pure as water from a well,
> Our hands made new to handle holy things,
> The source of all our seeing rinsed and cleansed
> Till earth and light and water entering there
> Gave back to us the clear unfallen world.
> . . . Was it a vision?
> Or did we see that day the unseeable
> One glory of the everlasting world
> Perpetually at work, though never seen
> Since Eden locked the gate that's everywhere
> And nowhere? . . .
> The shepherds' hovels shone, for underneath
> The soot we saw the stone clean at the heart
> As on the starting day. The refuse heaps
> Were grained with that fine dust that made the world;
> For he had said, 'To the pure all things are pure'.
> And when we went into the town, he with us,
> The lurkers under doorways, murderers,
> With rags tied round their feet for silence, came
> Out of themselves to us and were with us,
> And those who hide within the labyrinth
> Of their own loneliness and greatness came,
> And those entangled in their own devices
> The silent and the garrulous liars, all
> Stepped out of their dungeons and were free. . . .[10]

Here is a vision of the world transfigured. At first sight perhaps it may seem to be a transfiguration of some purely natural kind. We may object that the cleansing power which rinses and clears out perceptions at the beginning is said to spring up from the ground, not to descend from above, forgetting that earth no less than heaven is full of the activities of God's glory. But as we read on, we begin to perceive the source of this renewing light, which permits us to see 'the unseeable one glory of the everlasting world'. It is the presence with us of him who inspired the words, 'to the pure all things are pure',[11] and who said, 'If thine eye be single, thy whole body shall be full of light',[12] which enables us to see in garbage heaps, 'the fine dust that made the world' and which liberates the murderers, the thieves and all imprisoned in themselves, so that they are able to step out of their dungeons, to be with us and to be free. It is vitally important to notice that this is not only a vision of the natural world as full of the activities of God's grace. In the world of man no less than of nature, God's glory is to be seen, and often in the most unexpected, unlooked for places. Christ is present in the poor, the oppressed, the neglected, the forgotten. The theme of compassion is never far away from the theme of Christian praise.

Edwin Muir, in his humility, wondered at first how far his poem was Christian. It seemed to be about the transfiguration of the world in the presence of Christ, rather than about the transfiguration of Christ himself. It was only after its publication that he learnt how closely his own vision accorded with a great part of the teaching and experience of Eastern Christendom, in which for centuries, the Transfiguration has been interpreted in this very way. And this is not a poem of escape. The man who wrote it had not lived a sheltered, untroubled existence. In his adolescence he had worked in Glasgow, in a bone-manure factory of exceptional sordidness. He had passed through periods of deep and painful inner breakdown. In the years after the second world war, just before this poem was written, he had experienced the tragedy of the communist takeover in Prague. He knew the pain as well as the glory of life. The vision which he presents is one of God's creative and redeeming light at work in sorrow as well as joy, in darkness as well as glory.

We have looked at lines in which the Christian content is woven into the very texture of the poem. Now let us consider a passage from another poet, where the affirmation of the praise of God's glory is explicit and outspoken:

We praise Thee, O God, for Thy glory displayed in all the
    creatures of the earth,
In the snow, in the rain, in the wind, in the storm; in all of

Thy creatures, both the hunters and the hunted.
For all things exist only as seen by Thee, only as known by
    Thee, all things exist
Only in Thy light, and Thy glory is declared even in that
    which denies Thee; the darkness declares the glory of
    light.
Those who deny Thee could not deny, if Thou didst not
    exist; and their denial is never complete, for if it were
    so, they would not exist.
They affirm Thee in living; all things affirm Thee in living;
    the bird in the air, both the hawk and the finch; the
    beast on the earth, both the wolf and the lamb; the
    worm in the soil and the worm in the belly.
Therefore man, whom Thou hast made to be conscious of
    Thee, must consciously praise Thee, in thought and in
    word and in deed.

And Eliot goes on to enumerate the ways in which we can praise
God, laying the fire, sweeping the hearth, keeping house amidst a
cloud of witnesses. He speaks of God's mercies of blood and of
the death of the martyrs:

We thank Thee for Thy mercies of blood, for Thy redemption
    by blood. For the blood of Thy martyrs and saints
Shall enrich the earth, shall create the holy places.
For wherever a saint has dwelt, wherever a martyr has given
    his blood for the blood of Christ,
There is holy ground, and the sanctity shall not depart
    from it. . . .[13]

And, significantly, he mentions two of those holy places, Iona
and Canterbury, at the two extremities of the island of Britain.
Here we have a direct theological statement, a hymn of praise
growing out of one of the oldest and most universal of the hymns
of Western Christendom, the *Te Deum*. As in the previous poem,
the writer insists that it is not only the things which we normally
describe as beautiful which reveal God's glory. The conflict and
cruelty in the animal world is not evaded; we see the wolf and the
lamb, the hawk and the finch, the hunter and the hunted. Neither

is the conflict and cruelty in the human world ignored, the conflict which leads to the death of the martyrs. These are deaths which can only be understood in the light of the one death on the cross. In this above all God's glory is revealed. Here we have a powerful re-affirmation of the traditional belief that man must do centrally and consciously what all the rest of creation around him does unconsciously. In freedom and in knowledge, man is to praise God and so to realize the image and likeness in which he is made.

This is a theme which is wonderfully expressed in the songs and prayers of the Western Highlands. Perhaps nowhere else in Christendom is there such a moving expression of the sense of the all-pervasive presence of God with us, throughout the day and in every circumstance; a sense that even in the smallest details of life earth as well as heaven is full of God's glory. Preaching on Iona just over seventy years ago, George Congreve spoke of this with deep perception. In a sermon for St Columba's Day, 1908, he says 'I think you will find in this saint, and in the men formed by him, a remarkable confidence in nature, as a sphere which belongs to Christ by right, but waits for them to claim and hold for him indeed. They were not afraid of nature in her most dangerous moods; nor yet afraid of looking upon the seas and the rocks and the mountain pastures when the sun shone upon them, for fear they might love nature too much. Nature for them was not a questionable power, it was God's world, and they were God's children. . . . Nature could never become for them God's rival; or claim the heart in place of God, *for nature they recognized as the very kindness and love of God himself to men.*' [14]

This is not as we might perhaps imagine, some dreamy, romantic nature mysticism. The poems which we find in St Columba and in the tradition to which he belongs, come from men living a life of unremitting physical work, of constant mutual service within a tightly knit community, above all a life in which some hours every day would be given directly to the praise of God in the words of the biblical psalms.

Separated from God, the beauty of nature shuts us in silently. We have no means of communication through it with that which is beyond . . . But turning to God in our prayer, we find in God all its meaning, and we are set free. What was a closed door of mystery, prayer finds to be an open way to God. And now the revelation of God in nature burns itself into our thought, and awakens our love; *it flashes into joy of expression in our praise.*[15]

We think at once at St Francis of Assisi and of the Canticle of the Creatures, one of the greatest of all Christian hymns of praise to God, in and through his creation, as well as of the great Irish hymn known as St Patrick's breastplate.

If there is a poet who represents this tradition today, it is, I believe, Bobi Jones, the Welsh scholar and critic and writer, to whom we have referred in an earlier chapter. By theological conviction, a firm, indeed passionate Calvinist, his poetry overflows with the praise of God as his glory is revealed in all things; whether it is the growth of children, his love for his wife, the beauty of the countryside, the mystery of human creativity. There are not many poets whose vision of the world is so consistently and spontaneously sacramental. In his study of the religious significance of the Welsh literary tradition, *Llên Cymru a Chrefydd*, he is particularly illuminating about the poets of the fourteenth and fifteenth century, in many ways the golden age of Welsh poetic tradition. Their poetry is full of praise of the generosity and valour of the nobles, the warmth of their hospitality. They sing of beautiful women and the delights of illicit love. They celebrate the beauties of spring and summer, of hills and woods, and the woodland beasts and birds. But all this, as Bobi Jones maintains, has its roots in the praise of God as creator; only this gives it its true meaning. Only this reveals the true end and purpose of the writer, which is, in the end, the same as the true end and purpose of man, to glorify God and enjoy him for ever.

Writing of the greatest of all Welsh medieval poets, Dafydd ap Gwilym, Dr Jones says:

> Dafydd saw himself as singing the praise of God in his love songs no less than in his nature poetry. That is to say it is not God *in vacuo* who is the object of his praise, a God with only abstract or spiritual properties, but a Person who is seen concretely in his creation, and is to be praised with song as we rejoice in the work of his hands. No doubt Dafydd could understand the sense of separation from God which every creature experiences, and realized that there could be a tension between God and his

creation . . . but the more evident truth is just the opposite; the general grace of God is at work in the things of this world in a way which can be experienced definitely, gloriously. This is the theme of fully Christian praise.[16]

It has sometimes been suggested that the poetry of this period is to be understood primarily as the expression of a Christian platonism. Are the writers simply glorifying the ideal forms which lie behind the prosaic realities of every day? Professor Jones does not entirely reject the term Christian platonism, but he rejects any suggestion 'that the poets were monists, or believed that only the invisible forms were real and that the specific and unique was unimportant. Platonism, like many Eastern religions was other-worldly, holding the visible world to be an illusion. Christianity on the other hand holds together earthly and unearthly, phenomenal and noumenal, is at one and the same time historical and eternal.' [17] This quality he sees above all in the poets' love for the particular, the unique, and in their appreciation of the pleasures of the senses. The praise of God in and through all things, which we find in the simplicity of the popular traditions of the Western Highlands, can be paralleled in another idiom and another age, in the highly wrought, jewelled verses of the Welsh court poets, from whom Gerard Manley Hopkins, with whom we began, learnt much of his poetic technique. 'Christianity is at one and the same time historical and eternal', concerned with 'the intersection of the timeless with time', rooted in what is specific and unique, growing into something universal.

III

It is time to return from the poets to the theologians, and from our journeys into the North and West of Britain to come nearer to its centre. We come back therefore to the one theologian of unquestionably universal stature to be given to our Anglican tradition since the reformation, Richard Hooker. In his major work, *The Laws of Ecclesiastical Polity*, Hooker is concerned to defend the usages of the Book of Common Prayer from the objections of the

135

Puritans. Being a man who always sees the coherence of a subject, and who likes to trace everything back to first principles, his defence of the Prayer Book liturgy is bound up with his defence of the sacramental principle. This principle itself he always sees in relation to the Church's faith in the union of God with man in the incarnation of Christ our Lord.

Hooker's thought, complex and delicately balanced, is difficult to summarize. As a general introduction it is hard to improve on C. S. Lewis' account of it in the sixteenth-century volume of the *Oxford History of English Literature*, for in his scholarly works no less than in his popular writings, Lewis has a wonderful clarity of exposition. And here he is dealing with a writer who was no less important to him, as a Christian than as a literary historian. The 'mere Christianity' which Lewis expounded so forcefully in his popular books, owes much to Hooker's way of distinguishing essentials from inessentials, of looking behind the intricacies of a controversy to the heart of the faith. In his conviction that there is a central core of Christian faith and practice which will be recognised by Catholics and Protestants alike, which can be discerned without any illegitimate blurring of the issues, C. S. Lewis shows himself a true representative of the tradition which Hooker had done so much to create.

Because Hooker was concerned to defend what he believed to be the true rights of human reason and experience in certain areas of the Church's life, it has sometimes been thought that his theology has a secularizing tendency. Nothing, Lewis maintains, could be further from the truth:

Every system offers us a model of the universe; Hooker's model has unsurpassed grace and majesty. . . . Few model universes are more filled – one might say, more drenched – with Deity than his.

'All things that are of God' (and only sin is not) 'have God in them and he them in himself likewise,' yet 'their substance and his wholly differeth.' God is unspeakably transcendent; but also unspeakably immanent. . . . All good things, reason as well as revelation, nature as well as grace, the commonwealth as well as the Church, are equally, though diversely 'of God'. If 'nature hath need of grace,' yet also 'grace hath need of nature'. . . . We

136

must not think that we glorify God only in our specifically religious actions. 'We move, we sleep, we take the cup at the hand of our friend' and glorify him unconsciously, as inanimate objects do, for 'every effect proceeding from the most concealed instincts of nature' manifests his power. . . . We meet on all levels the divine wisdom shining through 'the beautiful variety of all things' in their manifold and yet harmonious dissimilitude.[18]

Here in a theologian, a philosopher, a jurist, a man of immense erudition, we find again the vision of the poet, the vision of God's glory to be seen at work in all things. Hooker was a man whose life had known a good deal of the turbulence and controversy of the reign of the first Elizabeth. His balanced and contemplative vision comes out of a society of seething energy and vitality, of great anxieties as well as great achievements. About this vision we may want to ask two things; first, where does it come from, and secondly, what does it mean in practice? In answer to these questions we can turn to John Keble, to the introduction to the critical edition of Hooker's works which he published in 1836, a vital year in the development of the Oxford Movement. It was this edition which brought Hooker's writings to the attention of nineteenth century England. Less brilliant a thinker than John Henry Newman, less massive a scholar than E. B. Pusey, it is easy to underestimate the importance of John Keble in the whole movement of renewal in nineteenth century Anglicanism. Yet Newman did not hesitate to call Keble 'the true and original author of the Oxford Movement'. To his deep intuitive sense of the interaction of Christian faith and life, all involved in the movement were deeply indebted. It was he who in himself stood for the continuity of the high church tradition through the barren years of the eighteenth century. And more than most people realized Keble too was a disciple of Hooker's. When he comes to ask what was the source of Hooker's way of seeing God's glory in all things, Keble turned to the early Christian writers and thinkers, those fathers of the Church to whom we have constantly had recourse in the course of this investigation:

The primitive apostolical men, being daily and hourly accustomed to sacrifice and dedicate to God even ordinary things, by mixing them up with Christian and heavenly associations, might well consider everything whatever as capable of becoming, so far, a means of grace, a pledge and token of Almighty presence and favour; and in that point-of-view might without scruple give the name of μυστήρια or sacraments to all those material objects which were anyhow taken into the service of religion; whether by Scripture, in the way of type or figure; or by the Church introducing them into her solemn ritual . . . God omnipresent was so much in all their thoughts, that what to others would have been mere symbols, were to them designed expressions of his truth, providential intimations of his will. In this sense, the whole world, to them, was full of sacraments.[19]

The constant memory of God, 'God omnipresent was in all their thoughts', enabled them to perceive all things as sacraments, potential moments of incarnation, moments in which we may be able to find the intersection of the timeless with time. It is in such a context that we can understand the specific sacraments of Christian worship, and see them in their true relationship to human life and experience as a whole.

Keble gives us here an account of the patristic view of the world itself as the sacrament of God's providential care, a view which is not afraid to affirm that God is present in all things. And he makes it clear that in this world we are not simply dealing with material copies of ideal archetypes. The picture is more dynamic than that. Objects and events are seen as meeting places, places where God comes out of himself to make his truth known, to reveal the content of his will; places where man can come out of himself in return to meet God, finding his daily life to be full of occasions for making over to God the happenings of everyday. The moral implications of this vision are as clear as its aesthetic consequences. We only have to consider the lines of a well-known hymn written at least ten years earlier than the Hooker preface, to see how deeply this way of looking at things had entered into Keble's attitude to life:

We need not bid, for cloister'd cell
Our neighbour and our work farewell,
Nor strive to wind ourselves too high
For sinful man beneath the sky:

The trivial round, the common task
Would furnish all we ought to ask;
Room to deny ourselves; a road
To bring us, daily, nearer God.[20]

'No doubt' as Keble himself allows, 'such a view as this har-
monizes to a considerable degree with Platonism; no doubt, again,
it has much in common with the natural workings and aspirations
of poetical minds under any system of belief', but in itself surely
it represents an expression of something basic to the Gospel, the
belief that already here and now, the kingdom of God is at hand,
present within us and around us, already leading us on towards a
fulness which as yet is only glimpsed. In all things, we can, if we
will, find God. It represents too the conviction that it is only in
the context of a world seen and experienced as sacramental at every
point, that we shall be able properly to understand and appreciate
the specific sacraments of the Gospel. As C. F. D. Moule puts it,
in our own day, 'It is theologically false, I am convinced, to
segregate the Gospel sacraments and the ecclesiastical sacraments
in any essential way (apart from degrees of authoritative institution)
from all those quasi-sacramental focal points of obedience in life
– the tangible, datable implementations of our will to serve God.
The convert at the penitents' bench, the repentant person making
restitution – these are using sacramental acts as channels for the
acceptance of God's gift of forgiveness.'[21] The water which we use
in baptism, the bread and wine which we bring to the Holy Table,
these are not random, isolated objects to be brought into Christian
worship half-apologetically. They are representative gifts, focal
points of a world known in faith to be in every part God's gift and
word to us.

IV

We have suggested throughout this book that the worship of almighty God needs to be seen in relation to the whole of man's life
in time and space, to be seen as the summing-up and making over
to God of all in this universe which is entrusted to man's care. This

139

certainly suggests that we should be encouraged to worship with the whole of ourselves, body as well as spirit, that the senses of sight and smell, feeling and taste, as well as hearing, have a place in our approach to God. It suggests that the form and ordering of the church building is not irrelevant to what goes on inside it, that we need not be afraid to make use of music and poetry, movement and colour. The mitigation, if not the abolition, of our fixed seating systems, our pews, would make it possible for congregations to discover what it is to move freely, to sit, to stand, to kneel, to lift up their hands in prayer and praise and to embrace one another in Christian greeting. There is much to be learnt in this area from charismatic Christians on the one side, and from the Eastern Orthodox on the other. In Orthodoxy, the body still plays an active part in worship; and the many and varied vehicles of the divine presence, not only the bread and wine which are consecrated, but also the painted icons, the Gospel book itself and many other blessed objects, complete and balance one another in a way which avoids undue concentration on any one focus of devotion.

But behind and beneath all such considerations there lies the belief that man is called to worship with the whole of himself and to bring the praises of all creation with him. Seen in this perspective it often seems that on the one hand our worship is insufficiently earthly, insufficiently rooted in the stuff of this world which God has given us, which man has so misused and which the natural sciences increasingly disclose to us. On the other hand it is often insufficiently heavenly, not enough open to the presence with us of the angelic powers of heaven, to the fact that our worship on earth is always joined with the worship of eternity. It is when the two are fused in one, when heaven and earth are united, in the union of man with God in Christ, that in the power of the Spirit the praise of all creation can break forth, and man can discover the purpose for which he was made. For as we see in the Epistle to the Romans, the creation itself is to be delivered from the bondage of corruption into the glorious liberty of the children of God. The Holy Spirit awakes in us and in all things an urgent hope of the consummation. As George Congreve put it, speaking on Iona:

> The solidarity of mankind with the whole creation is real. It is simply a fact that we are dust and return to dust. But St Paul

does not find our oneness with nature in the doom of a common death; he finds it in Christ the conqueror of death, and bids us look up to the throne of God to find the Eternal Son there, sharing in his glorified manhood the solidarity of all created things. As the Son of Man raised to the right hand of God gathers all mankind into blessing, or the possibility of blessing, so he heals the estrangement between man and nature, and lifts up to God both together in himself.[22]

In Christ's rising from the dead, we see not only the true destiny of humankind, but also the true destiny of all creation, lifted up, restored in him. In and with the whole creation, the fulness of man's restoration is made known. In this perspective we see something of the glory of God which is to be revealed.

So at the end of a book which has been very much concerned with the presence of the past, we find ourselves turned towards the future. The memory of God and of the deeds of God, proves to be something which liberates us now to live this present moment which God has given us, and which further enables us to look forward to the future in hope, the hope of the coming of his kingdom which even now is being made known in our world of flesh and blood.

Notes

Introduction

1 John E. Smith, *The Analogy of Experience: An Approach to Understanding Religions Truth* (Harper and Row 1973), p. 125

2 It is interesting to note that a man as well read as Eliot's friend, John Hayward, was ignorant of the book at the time when Eliot made use of it. Helen Gardner, *The Composition of Four Quartets* (Faber and Faber 1978), pp. 203–4

3 a. Brant Pelphrey, *Julian of Norwich: A Theological Reappraisal.* Unpublished thesis for the University of Edinburgh. 1976
b. Roland Maisonneuve, *L'Univers Visionnaire de Julian of Norwich.* Unpublished thesis for the University of Paris. 1978.
c. The critical edition by Edmund Colledge and James Walsh was published by the Pontifical Institute of Mediaeval Studies in Toronto, in 1978. (*A Book of Showings to the Anchoress Julian of Norwich*, two volumes)

4 T. MacFarland, *Coleridge and the Pantheist Tradition* (Oxford University Press 1969), pp. 161–2

5 Andrei Scrima in *Istina*, 1958, no. 3, p. 301 and p. 308

6 Philip Sherrard, *Constantinople. The Iconography of a Sacred City* (Oxford University Press 1965), p. 98

7. John E. Smith, *op. cit.*, p. 129

8. *The Prose Works of the Rt. Revd. Thomas Ken*, ed. W. Benham. (1853) p. 140

Chapter 1

1 S. Prickett, *Romanticism and Religion: The Tradition of Coleridge and Wordsworth in the Victorian Church* (Cambridge University Press 1976), pp. 145–6

2 *Selected Prose of T. S. Eliot*, ed. Frank Kermode (Faber and Faber 1975), p. 38 (italics not original)

3 *ibid.* p. 39

4 John Macquarrie, *Principles of Christian Theology* (Scribner, New York 1966), p. 67
5 Psalm 63:1–2 (I use the Book of Common Prayer numbering).
6 *St Francis of Assisi; Omnibus of Sources* (Franciscan Herald Press, Chicago 1973), p. 67
7 Psalm 107:6–8
8 Andrei Scrima, 'L'Avenement Philocalique dans l'Orthodoxie Roumanie; par Un Moine de l'Eglise Orthodoxe de Roumanie', *Istina*, 1958, p. 301
9 John 14:18

Chapter 2

1 Thomas Merton, *Conjectures of a Guilty Bystander* (Doubleday, New York 1968), p. 191
2 See the article by Dr Brant Pelphrey in *Sobornost*. Series 7, No. 7 pp. 527–535. It is greatly to be hoped that Dr Pelphrey's thesis, presented in the University of Edinburgh, will soon be published
3 *op. cit.* p. 192
4 Julian of Norwich, *Revelations of Divine Love*, trans. C. Wolters (Penguin 1973) p. 109
5 *ibid*. pp. 103–4
6 *St Erkenwald*, ed. Ruth Morse (D. S. Brewer 1975), p. 55
The authorship of the poem is disputed. It has been customary to attribute it to the same writer who produced *Sir Gawayne and the Green Knight, Pearl, Cleanness and Patience*. Its most recent editor, Ruth Morse, however has argued cogently against this attribution. I see the force of the argument from details of language and style, but still feel that the overall pattern of the poem, its theme and the genius with which it is handled, suggest the same hand as wrote *Gawayne*. The differences of style and language could perhaps be accounted for by the hypothesis that the work was written at a time when the poet was living in London, and therefore had a different audience in mind from that of his own native North West Midlands
7 Trans: *The Pearl Poet, His Complete Works*, ed. Margaret Williams (Random House, New York 1967), p. 306
8 *ibid*. p. 56. Trans: *ibid*. p. 308
9 *ibid*. p. 58. Trans: *ibid*. p. 311
10 *ibid*. p. 62–3. Trans: *ibid*. p. 317
11 *ibid*. p. 64. Trans: *ibid*. p. 319
12 William Langland, *The Vision of Piers Plowman. A Complete Edition of the B-Text*, ed. A. V. C. Schmidt (Dent Everyman 1978), pp. 14–5, Passus I, 148 ff. Trans: William Langland, *Piers the Ploughman*, ed. J. F. Goodridge (Penguin 1959), p. 36
13 *ibid*. pp. 122–123. XI. U. 140 ff. Trans: *ibid*. p. 131
14 *ibid*. pp. 124–125. XI. U. 179–188, 198–200. Trans: *ibid*. pp. 132–3
15 *ibid*. p. 220, XVIII. U. 22–3. Trans: *ibid*. p. 218
16 *ibid*. p. 221. XVIII. U. 57–61. Trans: *ibid*. p. 219. As A. V. C.

143

Schmidt comments in his recent edition, 'It is astonishing poetry, whether considered integrally or in the minutiae of such details as the strange haunting phrase 'leide hise eighen togideres', which comes with infinite gentleness after the majestic extended half-line preceding it.' (p. xviii)

17 *ibid.* p. 224. XVIII. 139–148. Trans: *ibid.* p. 221
18 *ibid.* p. 224. XVIII. 160. Trans: *ibid.* p. 221
19 *ibid.* pp. 225–6. XVIII. 172–189. Trans: *ibid.* p. 222
20 *ibid.* p. 226. XVIII. 202–3. Trans: *ibid.* p. 223
21 *ibid.* p. 230. XVIII. 315–327. Trans: *ibid.* p. 226
22 *ibid.* pp. 231–233. XVIII. 355–360, 362–373, 376–7, 394–399. Trans: *ibid.* pp. 227–8
23 Archimandrite Sofrony, *The Undistorted Image* (Faith Press 1958), p. 38
24 *The Lenten Triodion*, trans. Mother Mary and Archimandrite Kallistos Ware (Faber and Faber 1978), pp. 625 and 7
25 David McRoberts, *The Heraldic Ceiling of St Machar's Cathedral, Aberdeen.* (Friends of St Machar's Cathedral, Occasional Papers No. 2, Aberdeen 1976.)

Chapter 3

1 *The Works of George Herbert*, ed. F. E. Hutchinson (Oxford University Press 1953), p. 51
2 T. S. Eliot, *For Lancelot Andrewes, Essays on Style and Order* (Faber and Faber 1928), pp. 17–18
3 *ibid.* p. 140
4 *ibid.* pp. 29–30
5 Quoted in R. W. Church, *Pascal and Other Sermons* (London 1896), p. 62
6 *ibid.* p. 88
7 Lancelot Andrewes, *Works* L.A.C.T. Sermons Vol. I, p. 281
8 Thomas Merton, *Conjectures of a Guilty Bystander*, p. 12
9 Lancelot Andrewes, *Preces Privatae*, ed. H. Veale, 1899
10 A. L. Maycock, *Chronicles of Little Gidding* (S.P.C.K. 1954), p. 33
11 *op. cit.* p. 42
12 E. G. Selwyn, *The First Book of the Irenicum of John Forbes of Corse* (Cambridge University Press 1923), pp. 189–90
13 *ibid.* p. 212
14 Gilbert Burnet, *The Life of William Bedell, Bishop of Kilmore* (London 1685)
15 James Sibbald, *Divers Select Sermons* (Aberdeen 1658) p. 43
16 *ibid.* pp. 170–171
17 *ibid.* p. 147. We note how he is careful to let us know of the problems about the authorship of the Dionysian writings.
18 *The Funeral Sermons on the Death of Patrick Forbes, Bishop of Aberdeen* (Spottiswoode Society, Edinburgh 1845), pp. 125–8
19 *ibid.* pp. 153–4

20 *ibid.* pp. 155–6
21 *ibid.* p. 163
22 *ibid.* pp. 158–60
23 Aelred Squire, *Summer in the Seed* (S.P.C.K. 1980), see the note on pp. 229-30

Chapter 4

 1 V. E. Nash-Williams, *The Early Christian Monuments of Wales* (University of Wales Press 1950), pp. 123–5
 2 Charles Williams, *Taliessin Through Logres* (Oxford University Press 1969) p.18
 3 See the chapter 'Bronfraith Thomas Jones,' in R. M. Jones, *Llên Cymru a Chrefydd*, (C. Davies 1978).
 4 *Presenting Saunders Lewis*, ed. A. R. Jones and Gwyn Thomas (University of Wales Press 1973), p. 155
 5 'Les Devoirs des Catholiques Polonais envers Leur Culture Nationale et Religieuse', in *La Documentation Catholique* no. 1742, 21 Mai 1978, pp. 462–5
 6 St Maximus the Confessor, *Mystagogia*. Introduction and Commentary by Fr Dumitru Staniloae (Athens 1973, in modern Greek), pp. 182–3
 7 *ibid.* pp. 240–1
 8 See my study *Ann Griffiths*, in 'The Writers of Wales' series published by the University of Wales Press 1976
 9 This very popular hymn, the work of Titus Lewis (1773–1811) Baptist minister and shoemaker, is typical of the writing of the first century of the revival.
10 As to the writing of the golden age of Welsh poetry, the period from 1350–1500, I am glad to accept the judgement of two outstanding literary scholars, Mr. Saunders Lewis and Professor R. M. Jones, both of them distinguished poets and men of letters as well as eminent academics. In both, despite interesting differences of emphasis and approach, there is the conviction that the writing of this period is informed throughout by a deeply Christian sense of the world as God's world, and of human society as forming part of a whole coherent, ordered universe, in which the glory of God is at work. See Saunders Lewis, *Meistri'r Canrifoedd* and R. M. Jones, *Llên Cymru a Chrefydd*. There is a good introduction to this period in vol. II of *A Guide to Welsh Literature*, edd. A. O. H. Jarman and Gwilym Rees Hughes (University of Wales Press 1979)
11 St Maximus the Confessor, *Philosophical and Theological Questions, vol. I*. Introduction and Commentary by Fr Dumitru Staniloae (Athens 1978, in modern Greek), pp. 286–7 and p. 289
12 Gwenallt, *Ysgubau'r Awen* (Llandysul 1938), p. 85
13 Euros Bowen, *Poems* (Gomer Press 1974, in Welsh and English), p. 21
14 *op. cit.* pp. 144–5
15 *Ysgubau'r Awen*, pp. 24–5

16 *op. cit.* p. 42
17 *Presenting Saunders Lewis*, pp. 182–4
18 David Jones, *The Dying Gaul and Other Writings* (Faber and Faber 1978), p. 39. 'Perhaps Cymru has no shrines because she *is* one.'

Chapter 5

1 *Selected Prose of T. S. Eliot*, ed. Frank Kermode, p. 129
2 *ibid.* pp. 129–30
3 David Jenkins, *The Contradiction of Christianity* (S.C.M. Press 1976), p. 88
4 *Sobornost* Series 7, No. 1, Summer 1975, p. 31
5 Isaac de l'Etoile, *Sermons* (Sources Chretiennes), ed. Anselm Hoste, Vol. I, p. 191
6 Raimundo Panikkar. *The Vedic Experience*, (Darton, Longman and Todd 1977), p. xxxv
7 *ibid.* pp. xxxv–xxxvi
8 *ibid.* pp. 8–9
9 *ibid.* p. 13
10 *ibid.* p. 26
11 *ibid.* p. 28
12 *ibid.* pp. 781–2
13 *ibid.* p. 784
14 *ibid.* p. 831

Chapter 6

1 For the quotations from the *Four Quartets*, owing to the variety of editions, I have simply given references to the sections and line numbers in the various poems.
2 H. Blamires, *Word Unheard: A Guide Through Eliot's 'Four Quartets'* (Methuen 1969), pp. 110–11
3 'Ann Griffiths, a Literary Approach' by Saunders Lewis, in *Homage to Ann Griffiths* (Church in Wales Press 1976), p. 29
4 Mother Mary and Archimandrite Kallistos Ware, *The Lenten Triodion* (Faber and Faber 1978) p. 649
5 *ibid.* p. 647
6 *ibid.* p. 647
7 *ibid.* p. 625
8 *ibid.* p. 596
9 *ibid.* p. 628
10 *ibid.* p. 625
11 Good Friday Liturgy, *Roman Missal* (Burns and Oates 1961)
12 Julian of Norwich, *Shewings of Divine Love* adapted from the edition of Marion Glasscoe published by Exeter University in 1976
13 *The Agreed Statement on Eucharistic Doctrine* of the Anglican-Roman Catholic International Commission, Para. 11

Epilogue

1 Isaiah 6:3
2 Revelation 4:11
3 Revelation 5:13
4 Psalm 104:24
5 Revelation 5:12
6 Exodus 3:14, 15
7 *The Liturgy of St John Chrysostom*
8 'God's Grandeur' in *The Poems of G. M. Hopkins*, ed. W. H. Gardner and N. H. Mackenzie (Oxford University Press 1967), p. 66
9 cf. David Jones, *Epoch and Artist* (Faber and Faber 1973), p. 281. 'Something of this is, of course essential to all poetry for, if poetry is praise, as prayer is, it cannot co-exist with any malignant and persistent criticism of the nature of things . . . however much, superficially, the poet be a master-grouser, his theme a complaint, his mood dejected.'
10 Edwin Muir, *Collected Poems* (Faber and Faber 1964), 'The Transfiguration', pp. 198–9
11 Titus 1:15
12 St Matthew 6:22
13 T. S. Eliot, *Murder in the Cathedral* (Faber and Faber 1968)
14 George Congreve. *Christian Progress with Other Papers and Addresses* (Longmans Green 1913), p. 274 and p. 278 (my italics). Congreve was one of the earliest members of the Society of St John the Evangelist at Cowley, Oxford. For a time at the beginning of this century, Bishop's House on Iona was a house of the Cowley community. The island made a great impression on those of the brethren who stayed there. Father Benson's own remarkable poem, *St Columba*, is a product of these years. In the preface, he writes:

> 'We are not to think, however, of pioneer saints and missionaries as if they were raised up to satisfy the peculiar possibilities of bygone generations. The inner Christian life is the same from age to age, and unless we are living true to its requirements as they did, we cannot claim a vital participation in the inheritance of Christian life which they have bequeathed to us. The centres of ancient missionary movement, such as Iona and Canterbury, are not to be regarded merely with historic interest or the veneration of hagiology. We must feel them to be living with an inextinguishable flame which must perpetuate in our hearts its individual energy or shrivel us up in the doom of a nature incapable of responding to their glow.' It is not to be supposed that Eliot had read Benson's poem. But the conjunction of Canterbury and Iona in two so different writers is striking.

15 *ibid.* p. 279 (my italics)
16 R. M. Jones, *Llên Cymru a Chrefydd* (Swansea 1978), pp. 263–4
17 *ibid.* p. 273
18 C. S. Lewis. *English Literature in the Sixteenth Century* (Oxford University Press 1954), pp. 459–461

19 *The Works of Richard Hooker*, ed. John Keble (Oxford 1836), vol. I, pp. xci–xcii

20 John Keble, *The Christian Year*, 'The First Hymn'. As always, Keble needs to be read carefully even when apparently at his simplest. The rejection of monastic life in the first verse cited is more apparent than real. Keble was criticizing the romantic nostalgic mood of some of his contemporaries, who in fact had no intention of entering a monastery, since at that time there were none in the Church of England to enter. When in the course of the Oxford Movement religious communities of women began to come into existence Keble watched their growth with keen sympathy. In 1863 he preached a notable sermon at the annual festival of the Community of St Mary the Virgin at Wantage, in which he looked forward to the establishment of similar communities for men, which in fact followed in the foundation of the Society of St John the Evangelist at Cowley, three years later cf. A.M. Allchin, *The Silent Rebellion* (S.C.M. Press 1958), pp. 183–4

21 C. F. D. Moule. *The Sacrifice of Christ* (Hodder and Stoughton 1956), p. 55

22 *op. cit.* p. 259

Index

Gwilym, Dafydd ap, 88, 134–5

Hayward, J., 142
Herbert, George, 55–6, 62–3
Hilton, Walter, 4, 37
Hinduism, 102–7
historical sense, 24–5
Hooker, Richard, 56–7, 135–7
Hopkins, Gerard Manley, 128–9, 135
Hoste, A., 146
Hughes, G. R., 145
Hutchinson, F. E., 144
hymns, 84–8, 119–21

incarnation, 44–7, 60–1, 72–3, 111f
Isaac of Stella, 100
Isaac of Syria, St, 100
Islam, 101–2

Jenkins, D., 95, 146
John Chrysostom, St, 70, 71, 73–4
John-Paul II, Pope, 23, 84
Jones, David, 1, 33, 44, 93, 147
Jones, R. M., 91, 134–5, 145, 147
Judaism, 101
Julian of Norwich, 3–6, 9–11, 23, 38–40, 122, 143, 146

Keble, John, 6, 137–9, 148
Ken, Thomas, 17, 20–1, 142

Langland, William, 37, 44, 143
    Piers Plowman, 37, 44–54
Law, William, 5
Lewis, C. S., 136, 147
Lewis, Saunders, 81, 92–3, 119, 145, 146
Lewis, Titus, 145
Little Gidding, 62–3, 76
Liturgy of St John Chrysostom, 127–8
London, 41–3

MacFarland, Thomas, 11, 142
Macquarrie, John, 25–6, 143
McRoberts, D., 144

Maisonneuve, R., 142
Maurice, F. D., 20–1
Maximus, St, 85, 89, 98, 112, 145
Merton, Thomas, 38, 40, 61, 97, 112, 143, 144
monasteries, 6, 27–9, 31–3, 83, 133–4
Mosley, J. B., 59
Moule, C. F. D., 139, 148
Muir, Edwin, 130–1, 147
mysteries, 67–8

Nash-Williams, V. E., 79, 145
Nektarios of Aegina, St, 29
Newman, J. H., 6, 21, 137

Oxford Movement, 6, 14–15, 59, 137

Panikkar, Raimundo, 102, 146
    The Vedic Experience, 102–7
Pantycelyn, Williams, 87–8
Passion of Christ, 10, 47, 53, 120–1
Pelphrey, B., 142, 143
Pentecost, 16, 34, 53, 97, 122
Poland, Pastoral letter of the Bishops of, 84
prayer, 2–3, 19, 55–6, 59–63, 101f, 105–7, 113
Prickett, Stephen, 21, 142
provincialism, 95–7
Psalms, 126–7; liturgical use of, 27, 31–2
Pusey, E. B., 6, 21, 137

Quakers, 98

resurrection, 121–2, 141
Rolle, Richard, 4, 37
Rublev, Andrei, 98–9

sacraments, 67–8, 123, 139
saints, 23
Schmidt, A. V. C., 52, 143–4
Scrima, Andrei, 11–12, 34, 142, 143

Of related interest: